Praise for *The Powe*

"Plumeri illustrates his point with engaging anecdotes."

—*Success*

"Offers simple yet profound guidance on staying positive, motivating yourself and others, and achieving both personal fulfillment and professional success . . . Plumeri's story offers us all lessons for succeeding in all areas of life today. *The Power of Being Yourself* is an inspirational read for our times."

—800-CEO-READ

"After you finish this book, I am sure that you will agree with me that the country desperately needs a dose of Joe Plumeri. His passion, honesty, and sense of purpose flows through these pages, which are filled with life lessons that extend from his childhood to his rise to the top of the corporate world. Plumeri points out that the key to being a good public speaker or a successful leader is having the courage and self-awareness to be yourself—an important insight for all of us."

—Bill Bradley, former US Senator

"Joe Plumeri is truly one of a kind. In today's day and age, his message is an important one. This is the story of finding your passion, following your heart, but most of all: being yourself."

—Jeb Bush, former Governor of Florida

"Joe Plumeri's book is delightful. It is courageous in its honesty and profound in reminding us of what is most important in life. His references to Jack [Jackie Robinson] are heartening to me and further the message of brotherhood. I especially hope young people read it— to be inspired and to receive the guidance that so many of them are seeking in today's fast-paced world."

—Rachel Robinson, Founder, Jackie Robinson Foundation

"Joe Plumeri is one of the best motivators and leaders that I know. This book is his life story, both the heartaches he has faced and the many accomplishments he has had. Anyone interested in the art of leadership should read this book and, through Joe's career, learn some of the best traits possible."

—Henry Kravis, Co-Chairman and Co-CEO,
Kohlberg Kravis and Roberts (KKR)

"Wall Street has created a league of giants in the last half century and I regard Joe Plumeri as its Babe Ruth. Leading by doing it his way and leaving it all on the field. With Joe in our locker room, First Data is in the company of greatness, a genuine aura that comes shining through in *The Power of Being Yourself*."

—Frank Bisignano, Chairman and CEO, First Data Corporation

"A timely wake-up call in a world where heartless electronic communication too often takes precedence over genuine connection."

—In Business Greater Phoenix

"Challenges its readers to find their passion and pursue it with innovation and without fear."

—Italian America

"There is something irrepressibly guileless about the author. This makes him likeable, which demonstrates the power of being yourself, perhaps . . . Ultimately the stronger message is not about being your most authentic self, it is to pay attention to life beyond work."

—Financial Times

THE
POWER
OF
BEING
YOUURSELF

A GAME PLAN FOR SUCCESS—
BY PUTTING PASSION
INTO YOUR LIFE AND WORK

JOE PLUMERI

Da Capo
∞
LIFE
LONG

A MEMBER OF THE
PERSEUS BOOKS GROUP

Designed by Jack Lenzo
Set in 11 point Sabon by the Perseus Books Group

Cataloging-in-Publication data for this book is available from the Library of Congress.

ISBN: 978-0-7382-1829-8 (hardcover)
ISBN: 978-0-7382-1881-6 (paperback)
ISBN: 978-0-7382-1830-4 (e-book)

First Da Capo Press edition 2015
First Da Capo Press paperback edition 2016
Published by Da Capo Press
A Member of the Perseus Books Group
www.dacapopress.com

Note: The names and identifying details of people associated with events described in this book have been changed. Any similarity to actual persons is coincidental.

Da Capo Press books are available at special discounts for bulk purchases in the U.S. by corporations, institutions, and other organizations. For more information, please contact the Special Markets Department at the Perseus Books Group, 2300 Chestnut Street, Suite 200, Philadelphia, PA, 19103, or call (800) 810-4145, ext. 5000, or e-mail special.markets@perseusbooks.com.

10 9 8 7 6 5 4 3 2 1

Contents

Foreword by Joseph A. Califano Jr. vii
Prologue: The Boston Marathon Tragedy xiii

Principle 1: Everyone Has the Same Plumbing 1
Principle 2: Show the Way to Grandma's House 29
Principle 3: Cut Your Own Path 47
Principle 4: Let Sadness Teach You 69
Principle 5: Look Up, Not Down 95
Principle 6: Play in Traffic 121
Principle 7: Make Your Heart Your Teleprompter 147
Principle 8: You Gotta Have a Purpose! 169

Epilogue: I'm Not Done Yet 191
Applying the Principles 195
Acknowledgments 201
Index 203

V

Foreword

By Joseph A. Califano Jr.

I have always believed—and taught my children—that
the measure of a person's success in life is whether the
individuals and institutions that person engages are better off because of that engagement. That's what makes
Joe Plumeri so special and what makes this book so
important. From his upbringing on the streets of Trenton, New Jersey, throughout his life, up to the pinnacle
of national and international corporate leadership, the
people Joe has worked and competed with, agreed and
disagreed with, and laughed and cried with will tell you
how enriched they are from that experience.

How Joe Plumeri does it—his passion for life and
leadership, his ability to learn from tragedy, his uncanny
penchant for making impossible dreams come true—is
what his life and this book are about. For our nation
and people at a time when confusion and conflict can
blur the lines between right and wrong, when problems

seem intractable, when many individuals find obstacles insurmountable, Joe serves up the experiences and lessons of his life as a robust anthem of hope, just by being himself.

Remember the high hopes of the 1960s even amid all the trauma of those years: we were going to conquer poverty, provide health care for the elderly, make it so any kid could go to college, clean the air and water, put a man on the moon. In this new century we've traded hope for despair: cities go bankrupt, Washington is imprisoned in political gridlock, drugs threaten millions of our kids, the path of upward mobility seems too steep to climb, public schools fail to teach children how to read, write, and add. Too many people have reached the point of shrugging and saying, "It isn't even worth trying."

Joe Plumeri has an answer for those people. He says, "Of course it's worth trying, and you can succeed if you put your heart and your passion into it and dare to be yourself." The book you are about to read just might be the most important book you read this year because of the message Joe delivers: we must instill hope in our people again. We've got to have heart and learn to trust our instincts. We must start talking to each other. We need to start laughing. We need to rub up against each other, open up to each other, take a chance on connecting, get a sense of what it's like to walk in the other guy's shoes. And above all we need to find the strength and fortitude to be ourselves. If we have the courage to do these things, we can eliminate the scourge of hopelessness that haunts our national psyche.

When I went to work for President Lyndon Johnson as his domestic affairs aide, he said to me, "They tell me you're pretty smart, way up in your class at Harvard Law School. Well, let me tell you something: what you learned on the streets of Brooklyn will be a damn sight more helpful to your president than anything you learned at Harvard." LBJ was right. It's the same with Joe Plumeri. Joe learned a lot as a CEO of companies from New York to London, but what he learned on the street corners of Trenton about what makes people tick is going to be a far bigger help to our people than anything he learned in the corridors of executive suites.

Like all of us, Joe is human. He's made mistakes. But when he slipped, from that fall he learned not only how to get up but also what to do when he did. He revealed one of his mistakes as he chaired a banquet at the Pierre Hotel in New York when I stepped down as chair of CASA, the National Center on Addiction and Substance Abuse at Columbia University. The guest speakers included LBJ's eloquent daughter Luci Baines Johnson; Ben Bradlee, the storied editor of the

Washington Post; his wife, Sally Quinn; and the legendary lawyer Brendan Sullivan. Steve Kroft of *60 Minutes* was the master of ceremonies. But of all those sparkling stars the one that shone so brightly that it mesmerized the audience was Joe Plumeri.

Most everyone who was there remembers that night because of Joe. A black-tie dinner like this draws a pretty hard-nosed audience, with lots of jaded guests who keep talking at their tables during the speeches. But when Joe opened up from his heart about why he was chairing that dinner and why he was on the board of CASA, the audience, at first startled, was then suddenly so rapt that you could have heard hair grow. Joe told the story of his son Chris, all the troubles his boy had with anorexia and drug addiction, his child's years in and out of treatment, and how it all ended with Chris dying from an overdose before he reached the age of forty. Joe, his eyes tearing, told that room that he should have done more to try to be there for Chris. He wanted each of us to learn from his mistakes, to do all we could to be there for our loved ones, give them a hug, listen to them, make changes in our own lives so that our children, in turn, could be there for their loved ones and the people who matter to them. As he spoke, some guests cried. Some cried so hard they had to leave the room to compose themselves. Over the months since, many who were there that night told me Joe's talk had profoundly affected their own lives.

In this book, Joe Plumeri reminds us that human expressions of honest feelings and heartfelt emotions are characteristic of personal renewal. Joe's book tells his personal story to inspire and spark in you the kind of individual passion that will lead you to play your part in order to usher in a new day marked by hope and achievement.

Joseph A. Califano Jr. was President Lyndon B. Johnson's top White House assistant for domestic affairs from 1965 to 1969 and served as Secretary of Health, Education and Welfare from 1977 to 1979. He is founder and chair emeritus of the National Center on Addiction and Substance Abuse at Columbia University, an attorney, and the author of more than twelve books, including *The Triumph and Tragedy of Lyndon Johnson: The White House Years.*

Prologue

The Boston Marathon Tragedy

I t brought tears to my eyes when my son Jay told me he'd decided to run the 2013 Boston Marathon as part of a charity team. Jay wasn't a serious runner, more the kind to go jog a couple of miles now and then, but he was ready to run 26.2 miles that April 15 in memory of his brother. "That happens to be Chris's birthday," Jay told me. "This way I can run for Chris."

The race fell on what would have been Chris's forty-fourth birthday. He died suddenly in 2008 after years of battling a drug problem. Chris could have had his whole life in front of him. Losing him devastated our whole family. I think about my son Chris every single day and challenge myself to learn from the mistakes I made in not being there for him when he was growing up, not showing him I loved him, not spending enough time with him because I was too caught up in my career. Ever since then I have tried hard to be there for Jay, my

I was overcome with tears when my son Jay told me he planned to run the 2013 Boston Marathon in memory of his brother Chris—and in tears again on race day when I hugged Jay on the race course. Later that day, the bombs went off. *Image courtesy of Joe Plumeri*

younger son, and Leslie, my daughter, in ways that I could not for Chris.

There was no way I was going to miss watching Jay run in this marathon for Chris. We made it a family outing. Jay was on the course running with "CJP" painted in black on his arm for Christian Joseph Plumeri, and Leslie and I roamed around, taking in the scene in Boston. The day was beautiful, with the sun shining, the temperature climbing into the mid-fifties, and an electric buzz of excitement building among the crowd along the course. People were cheering and chanting, smiling and laughing. There were people out there running who were seventy and eighty and ninety years old! I saw people running as Roman warriors with helmets and shields. I saw one person running as a hot dog. I saw another running as a hamburger. You know that expression, "Dance like nobody is watching" These people were *running* like nobody was watching. Talk about being yourself!

I was struck to notice that most were running for someone else, not themselves. They held up signs like "Friends of Griffin" or "God bless Sally." I did a double-take when I saw two people running together, one with a hand on the shoulder of another. What was going on there? It turned out there were blind people running! Can you imagine not being able to see and running 26.2 miles? Or running 26.2 miles strapped to a blind person to lead them the whole way? Up front they had people in wheelchairs with someone running along pushing them for 26.2 miles. One guy was running along pushing a specially built wheelchair with an arrow that read, "This is my son."

None of it was about running. It was about who these people were. It was about grit and spirit and heart. It was about being fulfilled by setting and reaching a goal, no matter how crazy it might have seemed, and it was about helping others to reach their goals. The context happened to be a marathon on a beautiful New England day in April. The real meaning of the event was the passion and the heart and the commitment and the dedication people were showing.

Leslie and I found a spot near the Mile 15 marker in Wellesley to wait for Jay, and when we spotted him the joy I felt was indescribable.

"This is for Chris, Dad," Jay called out. "This is for Chris."

I started to cry. How could I not? Leslie snapped a picture of the two of us together, me briefly matching stride with Jay. Then we waved him on his way and were on the move, eager to find a spot as close as we could get to the finish line. Leslie and I worked our way through the crowd and paused in front of the Lenox

Hotel, which is on Boylston Street, about half a block from the finish line. We took in the action from there for a while, but the crowd was piled about six deep, so I thought we could do better.

"It's going to be a while before Jay finishes," I told Leslie. "Let's try to move up."

The finish line was full of small wonders. A couple behind us started to cry when they saw their daughter finish. Some of the runners would get to the finish line and lift their arms up like they were Rocky running up the steps of the Philadelphia Museum of Art. You could almost hear the *Rocky* theme swelling in the background. Again and again, as someone approached the finish line, the big crowd would roar its approval, and you could see how the exhausted runner fed off of the energy. There was such joy in the air, such a feeling of ecstasy; you could inhale it and be filled up by it.

Leslie and I were making good progress walking over toward the finish line until we came up on bleachers that blocked our way. We were stuck, but only for a minute. That was when the first bomb went off. It was so close, only one hundred yards from where we were standing. I could smell it. Explosives have a very distinct smell, which I knew from my days in the army. I grabbed Leslie, and we started to run. Then the second bomb went off where we'd been standing a few minutes earlier near the Lenox Hotel. I looked around us and saw severed limbs and carnage all around and heard the screams and the moans and the yells.

"Dad, there's a leg there and an arm there," Leslie said, pointing.

Tears of ecstasy and celebration had turned to tears of horror. Everywhere you looked there were people who had been injured, and I didn't see a single person who was hurt who was not being attended by someone. Random people in the crowd were doing what they could to help. There were runners draped in plastic sheets after finishing who didn't have cell phones and couldn't find their loved ones amid all that chaos; people all over were helping strangers get in touch. In the middle of the horror and chaos I was inspired to see the way people joined together to help each other, the way even tragedy can bring people together. Even in agony I saw the best in people.

I was frantically looking for Jay. Never in my life was I so happy that he was a slow runner! I knew he was at least three or four miles away when the first blast hit, but at a time like that, when nothing makes sense, my mind started to go haywire on me. What if I had it wrong? Or what if he'd suddenly turned into Alberto Salazar and run like a gazelle the last few miles and finished ahead of schedule? What if somehow he'd been hurt? What if he'd been taken from me? Even if I logically knew it was crazy to think like that, the thought of losing another son had me in a panic. I said to myself, *God can't be that cruel.* I walked up and down Commonwealth Avenue, past runners in their capes looking like refugees. I must have walked fifteen miles searching for Jay. He didn't have his cell phone, so we had no way of connecting. Where could he be? If I saw a policeman, I would ask where they were sending runners who could not finish because of the blasts. I asked strangers on the street. I asked anyone I could.

I kept looking at my phone, hoping for good news, and finally got a text message from a number I didn't recognize. It said, "heading for the ritz." Could it be from Jay? If so, it was a very casual-sounding message. I called the number and got the voicemail of a girl named Jenny. Maybe Jay had asked to borrow someone's cell phone to text me? Only one way to find out: I hurried over to the Ritz, and there was Jay, casually sipping a beer. In the confusion of everything that had happened he hadn't watched any video of the aftermath of those bombs going off; I hugged him and cried joyous tears to feel my own flesh and blood alive and well, but even when I tried to tell him about all I'd seen that day, it didn't really connect for him.

Then, the next morning, he finally watched some news reports and the full magnitude of the tragedy hit him, and he called me to tell me about it.

"Holy shit, Dad!" he said. "I just saw what happened."

They say when you're about to die your whole life flashes before you. I had the feeling that day of every emotion known to mankind flashing over me. In seconds I went from ecstasy to agony, and everyone in the crowd did too. I felt every human emotion. It was breathtaking from the ecstasy and the joy of being with my daughter, being with my son, seeing my son run for my son, and all the emotions that go with that. More than anything that day made me feel lucky: I was lucky my son Jay was not hurt in any way. I was lucky Leslie and I moved when we did and were not hurt. If I'd have lost her, I don't know how I'd have ever found a way to move on after that. I was lucky I got to see such powerful glimpses of human good in the reaction of all the people after the explosions ripped us all loose from any sense of reality. But I was also lucky I had those great hours before the acts of madness turned everything upside down—the beautiful day and the inspiration of seeing people running for other people.

That day was a reminder of the difference between ideas you pack into your head, like slogans, and the core truths we know in our hearts and carry with us every day, whether or not we choose to listen. Life is a great teacher, and different periods of my lifetime have taught me different principles, which I will do my best to convey over the course of this book. It was a day that reinforced for me how the richest and most joyful emotions are connected with sadness and disappointment and that if we want the good stuff, we might open ourselves up to some sorrow. If we want to cry tears of joy—and who doesn't?—then we might also need to shed some tears of sadness. Through those tears we are more ourselves. Through those tears we live life more joyously and more fully. We have a better shot at nurturing the relationships that matter to us in life and being there for people, not failing them as I failed my son Chris all those years ago.

But it goes beyond that: if we can live in the moment and be honest and true in our emotions, that carries over into how we live all facets of our lives, including how we do our jobs. We live in a world of people without heart or vision, getting by on following the status quo, the statistical analysis, the robotic stuff that has everything to do with what's easy and nothing to do with what's right. The heartless too often takes precedence. Texting and e-mail are impersonal. Leaders of business and politics too often base their key choices on impersonal polling data or the impersonal advice of consultants.

> If we can live in the moment and be honest and true in our emotions, that carries over into how we live all facets of our lives, including how we do our jobs.

Let me ask you a question: Why is it that we live in a culture where being authentic and human is always celebrated, and yet when someone is human enough to shed a tear, they feel they need to apologize? People say they had to "fight" the tears. Why in the hell are they *fighting* back tears, like it's a criminal offense, like it's a felony to cry in public? They talk about almost "losing" it. What have you got to lose by being honest and true and human? What is it about our culture that makes that disallowed except at a funeral or a wedding or a catastrophe? You won't find anybody who says they don't like authenticity and keeping it real. And yet they apologize for crying.

The golfer Fred Couples gave a great speech when he was inducted into the PGA Hall of Fame in 2013. Fred was talking about one of his mentors, "Supermex" Lee Trevino, who helped him out when he was young. At one point Fred had to stop speaking because he was on the verge of tears. He found his way forward, and then toward the end of the speech he interrupted his prepared remarks and blurted out, "This is the coolest night of my life!" and openly broke into tears, raised his arms in triumph and walked off the stage. I loved it! That was a human

> People say they had to "fight" the tears. Why in the hell are they *fighting* back tears, like it's a criminal offense, like it's a felony to cry in public?

moment. He didn't mind showing the world who he was. I choked up watching at home and felt great crying along with Freddy. He's usually a cool customer, but this time he was overcome and he showed it, and that gave a glimpse of the authenticity of the guy, who I always liked.

Yet crying is seen as a show of weakness or as a sign of having no discipline. People seem to believe it's somehow a bad thing. It offers a glimpse of their true identity that they would rather hide from the world. But nobody has a problem with expressing themselves in an e-mail or a text. I really believe people will say things they wouldn't say in front of you because you're not there to see their reaction. You're not there to be the recipient of their wrath. How many people now use texts or e-mails to fire someone? Or to ask for a divorce? Why do they do that? They do it because they don't want to be there to see someone's emotional reaction. So we're only authentic when we're writing an e-mail or a text because the person is not there when someone is reading. We are becoming more and more an inauthentic society.

I'm no swami. I'm no guru. I'm a guy from New Jersey who talks like a guy from New Jersey—with my hands, sure, but also with my heart. I'd like to encourage you to join me in trying to get back to what matters. This is a book to apply in your life and work. I've been a CEO for years. I've made a lot of tough choices and learned from them. I've made a ton of mistakes and done my best to learn from each and every one of them as well. I could do a book focused only on making good choices in the business world, but I want to aim higher. I want to write a book for everyone—and I'm betting I can make you laugh, make you cry a little, and, above all, inspire you. I'm gonna give it my best shot anyway. I'm gonna take a regular-New-Jersey-guy approach to talking us all past the cloud of fear and hate and sourness that hangs over the country. All the things that inspire us most—self-sacrifice, generosity, courage, and hope—are qualities in short supply these days. Everybody's a robot. Everybody's too scared, too busy, or too stressed to be human.

How can we regain our bearings? I say it's simple enough: listen to your heart and share what it's telling you with anyone you can. Leave fear and worry aside, and step into the full light of joy and happiness. That's how you find it in you to be yourself. And let that be enough—more than enough. I've been able to follow my passion in life and make that work for me beyond my wildest hopes or expectations or dreams. I'm a person who feels what I feel, all the way, and I wouldn't want it any other way. I laugh more than a lot of people do. I smile more than a lot of people do.

And I shed a tear or two more than a lot of people do too—especially most other men. That's how it is when you live your passion—you follow it and you feed it. The passion isn't just a fixture in your life; it *is* your life, and it *is* who you are. You can't do passion halfway. That's not passion. Living your passion means you're all in. You trust your heart and trust your gut, wherever that takes you. You savor the joy and the hope and that feeling you have when you know you've left everything on the field and given it your all.

> You can't do passion halfway. That's not passion. Living your passion means you're all in. You trust your heart and trust your gut, wherever that takes you.

Feeling strong emotion, even sadness, tells you you're alive. It proves you're tuning into your passion loud and clear. Passion is something every single person has or can have. Even if they've got problems, even if they've had it up to here with their job or their marriage or their whatever, still they can find passion in their lives. It might take a little work, a little courage and patience, but if they nose around and get down to it, there is some part of their life where they can find it. If you've lost your passion, find it! You know it's there somewhere. Keep looking. You've got to find it, because if you don't have that deeper emotional connection to your life, professionally, personally—*somewhere* in your life—then you're hollow. There is nothing that can ever truly satisfy you. There is no purpose. Living your passion is not only the best way to feel good and feel engaged, to feel excited and powerful, but it is also the best way to keep your bearings when all about you others are losing theirs. It will make you happier, and it will make you better.

Everyone Has the Same Plumbing

Wall Street is an insular world. If you spend decades in that corporate culture as I have, you can start to think you're not able to connect with people from other places, especially far-off places and foreign countries—people there talk funny; they have different ways. But my time in London working for the insurance broker Willis starting in 2000 reminded me that when you come right down to it, we all have the same plumbing. Before that time I would tend to think of English people and German people and French people as being somehow strange and unknowable, but not after my time at Willis.

The September 11, 2001, attacks had an impact on all of our lives. That's a given. But I think we could have learned more from the events of that day and their aftermath. People from Alaska to Alabama were all glued to their TV sets. Everybody felt united in their sense of anguish and grief. We cried together for the victims of the terrorist attacks on the World Trade Center and on the Pentagon in Washington, and we cried some more for their families and cried some more for ourselves and what we all lost that day. Those tears brought us together. They made us all feel united in being Americans.

But the rest of the world was watching as well. From the first moments after the news broke of the two planes slamming into the Twin Towers people around the world made clear that they saw the attacks as attacks also on them. French president Jacques Chirac declared, "In these appalling circumstances, the whole French people, I want to say here, is beside the American people." The leading French newspaper, *Le Monde*, never shy about following an anti-American line, trumpeted a front-page headline declaring, "*Nous sommes tous Américains*"—We are all Americans. The British were so moved that the Queen gave the order to play the "Star-Spangled Banner" during the ceremonial changing of the guard at Buckingham Palace. The largest gathering in the world honoring the victims of the September 11 attacks who died in New York,

Washington, and Pennsylvania was actually the one that took place in Berlin, Germany, where more than two hundred thousand people gathered in the city's storied Tiergarten Park to cry together during a performance of "Amazing Grace," and the German President, Johannes Rau, cried out, *"Amerika steht nicht allein!"*—America does not stand alone.

Many of my friends were killed when the Twin Towers crumbled. I was devastated. But you know what? I was surrounded by people who also were devastated—and I happened to be in Copenhagen that day. All around me were Danish people who had never even been to New York, had never set foot inside the World Trade Center, and these people were as sad as I was. I watched them cry all around me. I kept thinking to myself, "These people are not even Americans, and they're crying too." Everybody truly was an American that day.

As a New Yorker abroad, I was blown away by the reaction of the Danes that day. It's so true that the things that unite us as people are far more important than the things that divide us, no matter where we were born, no matter where we live. But why does it need to take wrenching sadness to bring us together? Can't we also be joined by tears of joy? Can't smiles and laughter also draw us together?

Looking back, I can't help but wish I had seen the tragedy as a wakeup call to focus less on my career advancement and more on getting back to being there for my family, for Chris and my other kids. Deepak Chopra, who once taught at Harvard Medical School and later became a spiritual leader in California, might actually have made the statement on September 11 that I most wish I had thought about more at the time: "For me and my family personally, September 11 was a reminder that life is fleeting, impermanent, and uncertain," Chopra said. "Therefore, we must make use of every moment and nurture it with affection, tenderness, beauty, creativity, and laughter."

I don't talk fancy like Deepak Chopra. But his words track closely with my message here in this book: Why not spend every minute of the day staying open to the idea that, with a smile or a kind word or a well-timed action, you can make someone else feel good? You can lift them up a little? Help them laugh instead of scowl or frown? Smiles and laughter bring people together, which can be more than nice; it can also inspire good teamwork and communication and that indefinable deeper sense of common cause that makes all the difference in making something happen with a company or in life. The main thing is to have the courage and the faith to be yourself. If you know you're going to do the work and you have the talent and the drive, you don't need to worry about putting on a mask or trying to act like a robot; you can relax and let a little spontaneity and joy into your days.

It took uprooting myself to London for me to have a real moment of questioning myself on some of these basic beliefs of mine. I'm serious. I almost did—for a minute. There was something about that whole British stiff upper lip thing that could throw you off. They came across at first glance as so proper and so very *English*. It's human nature that when people are different, our first reaction is to see superficial differences as mattering more than they really do.

> The main thing is to have the courage and the faith to be yourself. If you know you're going to do the work and you have the talent and the drive, you don't need to worry about putting on a mask or trying to act like a robot; you can relax and let a little spontaneity and joy into your days.

Here's how it unfolded: I was with my first wife, Nancy, in Paris. I'd left Citigroup at the end of 2000 after thirty-two years, figuring I'd done all I could do there and a change would do me good, but a change to what? I didn't know. So I signed up for a trip to France sponsored by the College of William and Mary, my alma mater—a hike through Burgundy, a boat ride along the Seine in Paris, and a visit to Roland Garros Stadium for the French Open. The night before the boat ride Nancy and I took a little walk starting at the Hotel Bristol, where we were staying, along the Rue du Faubourg-Saint-Honoré, right past the Élysée Palace, where the French president lives. As we were walking along window shopping, we ran into Henry Kravis, who had become a partner at Bear Stearns at age thirty and went on to create the leveraged buyout business, becoming a founding partner of Kohlberg, Kravis, Roberts & Co., known as KKR. Henry and I had met earlier in the year through Lew Eisenberg, a great friend of mine for more than twenty years who has one of the biggest hearts of anyone I've ever known.

Henry knew I'd left Citigroup. "What are you going to do with yourself now?" he asked.

"I'm looking for my next adventure!" I said.

We laughed at that, and I figured that was the end of it, but then Nancy piped up. "Maybe you can find him a job," she said to Henry.

It was a throwaway line, a mere pleasantry, but it got Henry thinking. "I've mentioned a company we have that could be a good fit, Willis, a global insurance broker headquartered in London."

I had no interest. Insurance? London? To me the commercial insurance industry was way too stodgy, and for a Jersey guy like me, London was not quite my neighborhood.

"I'll call you," Henry told me. "We can talk about it."

"Sure," I said.

What was I going to tell the man? No? True, I had zero interest in getting into the insurance business in London. Talk about your fish-out-of-water stories. I'm a New Jersey guy, a New York guy. But being gracious only made sense. Henry owned a lot of companies, and I was looking for a job.

"Why don't you go to London?" Henry suggested later. "You can talk to the chairman you'd be replacing. It might be awkward, but it will give you some insight."

Again, what was I going to say? No? You don't say no to Henry Kravis. I have known a lot of great businessmen, worked with them and had them as friends, and there is no one in business I respect as much as Henry, both as a man and as a businessman. I can go on and on and say all kinds of nice things about him, but I'll just stop at that.

"This is a great opportunity," I told my wife.

The opportunity I had in my sights was a visit to Omaha Beach, Normandy, where so many young US GIs gave their lives in one of the critical battles of World War II, D-Day. I'm a great history buff, and I'd never been to Normandy. But the weather played hell with my plans. I'd paid to take part in an amphibious landing at Normandy, just to reenact, but it was so stormy and windy that it wasn't possible and we had to take a plane instead. It didn't matter. That is a trip every American ought to make. We went to the World War II museum in Caen, France, and to the Battle of Normandy Memorial Museum in Bayeux. When you see the scale of those cliffs, it makes you feel very inadequate just thinking of all those eighteen- and nineteen-year-old kids getting gunned down as they headed up those massive cliffs at Omaha Beach. I cried all day.

My visit to the Willis offices in London was bound to be a letdown after the adrenaline rush of that visit to Normandy Beach. Willis was located in a stately old structure at 10 Trinity Square right across from the Tower of London called the Port of London Authority Building, a lavish, five-sided building built by David Lloyd George after World War I in the Beaux-Arts style.

"Yes, sir, how can I help you?" said the guard in a blue jacket who greeted me.

I gave him my name and said I was there to see the chairman.

"Yes, the chairman," he said. "Please follow me to the chairman's lift."

The chairman's got his own lift? You're kidding me. This was totally foreign to my idea of leadership. The chairman needs to talk to other people, not be shut away in his own lift. When we got off on the second floor, I saw that all the fancy doors were closed.

"Who else has offices on the second floor?" I asked the fellow in the blue jacket.

"Oh, just the chairman," he said, as if it were terribly amusing to imagine that anyone else might be allowed to work on the same level as the exalted chairman.

I was left waiting in the reception area—and waiting and waiting. No one greeted me. No one came out to ask whether I wanted some water or a cup of coffee. I was just left to cool my heels. I had a long time to study the ornate oak, walnut, and mahogany paneling. Finally he came out. I almost had to laugh to look at the way he was dressed—impeccably of course, but so very starched. White collar, blue shirt, white cuffs, cuff links, and, as a matter of fact, he even had on a jacket with one of those chains hanging down from his lapel. What in the heck are those for?

I was expecting at least some formal British version of small talk—how are you, have you enjoyed London on your visit—but not from this guy.

"Let's talk about Willis," he said, the first words out of his mouth.

I could have played along. I thought of playing along. But no, it all felt wrong, and I don't like it when things feel wrong. I had to be me. I had to try to get back some sense of balance.

"How ya doin'?" I asked him, flashing a big smile.

That threw him off, my introducing something personal into the conversation. He stared at me a minute, blinking, the way you look at a bug that's landed on your plate of strawberries and cream. He did not answer my question.

"I don't think KKR should hire you," he said.

Up until that moment I had absolutely no intention of taking the job. I knew nothing about London and nothing about the commercial insurance industry. But this guy had turned me like a dime. He was so sure I couldn't do it that I was suddenly very intrigued by the idea of proving him wrong.

"And why shouldn't they hire me?" I asked him, kind of playfully.

I was messing with him, but I don't think he even knew.

"You don't have any insurance brokerage experience," he informed me stiffly, as if any of this was news to me. "You don't have any international experience. And no one from outside of Britain has ever run this company."

"I think you're wrong about the international experience," I told him with a straight face. "I have international experience."

"Of what international experience do you speak?" he asked.

"I have relatives living in Sicily!" I told him.

Not even a flicker of a smile. Not a laugh. No sign of life from this guy at all. He was so superior and so

nasty, and he challenged my competence and my profes-
sionalism, my leadership and my experience. He even
challenged my pride as an American!

"I think I have some interest in pursuing this," I
told KKR just as soon as I could.

He could have made me go away just by being civil.
He didn't. Instead he riled me up. I agreed to take the job
and rented a flat in London. Even before I was officially
announced as the new chairman in mid-October 2000, I
took to the phones in a move that was completely unprece-
dented. I got a list of the top one hundred executives in the
company and called them one by one to introduce myself.
Some of the conversations were out-and-out hilarious—
these people were so shocked to be hearing from me.

"Hi, this is Joe Plumeri," I'd say.

"Yeah, and I'm Joe DiMaggio," came the sarcastic
reply, or countless variations on that.

But more often there would be dead silence on the
other end.

"I just want to introduce myself," I'd continue, "and
tell you I'm looking forward to working with you as the
new chairman. We're going to build a great company
together!"

Some of them would just cough nervously. They
were all incredulous.

"Well, thank you, yes, yes, thank you," was about
all they could squeeze out in reply.

Word got around that this new guy was different. Which I clearly was. My predecessor never came out of his office, his door was always closed, he had his own lift, and he didn't want anyone working on the same floor as him. Here I was, calling people one by one and just trying to be friendly and upbeat, even though that was difficult, especially when I called Vic Krauze in the Minnesota office. He almost hung up on me.

"This is one of those New York stock brokers making a cold call, isn't it?" he asked me. "I'm tired of this shit."

"No, it's Joe Plumeri," I told him. "I'm the new chairman and CEO of Willis."

Imagine his embarrassment later when he found out it was really me—and that I used to be a stock broker. It was a double dose of embarrassment. He called me back to apologize. He was mortified. I laughed the whole thing off. I was enjoying myself. It's great fun to take peoples' expectations and stand them on their head. I was dealing with a company culture that saw the CEO as a figure who mixed with the regulars about as often as Marie Antoinette did. So the mere fact of me making those calls, just to reach out to people and set a positive tone, was a landmark and created quite a buzz.

Then came the day for the big Monday meeting when my predecessor could begin his farewell tour by addressing Willis's top two hundred people in London, gathered in the Tower Room of the Port of London Authourity Building, with its history of hosting a famous UN reception back in the 1940s. The previous chairman and I were up in the front, and he was sitting down at his desk, looking down at the pages of his speech. Then he started reading. Without standing up. Without looking up. Was he *trying* to make me look good by comparison?

"I would like to introduce the new chairman and CEO of Willis," he continued in the same monotone, like a secretary reading off minutes of a previous meeting, and added that I was a man who has no insurance experience and no international experience, so I was going to need a lot of help from all of them.

To this guy, it was clear, anyone like me had two strikes against him: I was from the working class and I was an American. Surely I was doomed to fail. At that moment he introduced me I actually froze for a moment. It was nothing anyone else would have noticed, just instantaneous, but I did doubt myself briefly. I was looking out on this room full of people all sitting so erect and perfect, with their suits and ties all just so, not a thread out of place. I didn't see anyone smile. The mood in the room was just so serious. There was an anxiety in the air, and they were staring up at me with looks of appraising curiosity, wondering: Who is this guy?

I had just a few seconds to decide who I was. Was I going to be stiff and stuffy? Was I going to go the blend-in route and give a speech consistent with what I thought their expectations were? Or was I going to throw all that out the window? Was I going to go with my heart and lighten the place up? Was I going to give them full-frontal Joe Plumeri?

I'm guessing you know which direction I took. I stood up, peeled off my jacket, and bolted away from my predecessor so I could work the room, kick up some enthusiasm, and generate some smiles and excitement. They thought they were under attack. This was their worst nightmare: Fonzi had arrived on their little island and was terrorizing them.

"Here at Willis we have a great history," I said, enjoying shocking them with my upbeat delivery and blunt American accent. "But you know what? Forget all that. We don't want to live by tradition. We want to build on it. We shouldn't let tradition be our jailer. We don't care anymore about being the oldest insurance broker in the world. We don't care about that history. We want to focus on the here and now and on the future. We have a great future to look forward to. We're going to do great things together. Some day Willis stock is going to be traded at thirty dollars a share! Or forty dollars a share!"

They thought I was out of my frickin' mind. Really, I think many of them would not have been surprised if guys in white jackets burst into the room about then and tried to haul me off to a room with padded walls. I was talking about the stock hitting forty bucks a share, and at the time it was a private company and there was *no* Willis stock. But you know what? I got them jacked up. They were excited! Willis went public not long afterward and, last I checked, was trading at right around forty-two bucks a share.

If I wasn't myself then and there, how was I ever going to be myself? The choice I faced that day in London was one that I had never confronted in my entire life because I had always operated in the United States on my home turf. That was a defining moment for me. I got their attention and accomplished what I wanted to in two ways: they not only had a very vivid sense of who I was and what they were getting in their new CEO but, beyond that, they also saw without a shadow of doubt that the old ways were out the window, that it wasn't going to be business as usual, same old, same old.

Changing cultures takes time and takes patience. But I had at least started to make some inroads. What I tried to do was to bring pride into the organization again. I wanted to give them a sense of who they were and how they could regain their rightful place. At the time everybody thought Willis was unenergetic with no vision and no direction, just an old British insurance broker, and that meeting was the turning point. Earlier on, KKR enlisted the help of other insurance companies that invested in Willis along with KKR because it was in their interest to have another large broker. But if it were only the large brokers, Marsh and Aon, who were dominating the market, that was bad for everyone else. So in my meetings and discussions I kept hearing we were the third alternative.

"We are not *alternative*, ladies and gentlemen!" I said in that speech. "This company does not exist to be an *alternative*. This company exists to be the greatest broker in the world. I'm tired of hearing people say that we are the third alternative. We are not a third alternative. We don't get up in the morning to be an alternative. We get up in the morning to be the greatest broker in the world. People say insurance is a boring business? Insurance is the DNA of capitalism! You can't do anything without insurance. No airplane would fly without insurance. No building would ever be built. No employee would ever be hired. What we're doing here matters!"

A lot of my colleagues had invested their own money in the leveraged buyout, at three dollars a share, and were hoping to see that climb to six or nine. On June 12, 2001, we took the company public at $13.50 a share. The first tick on the New York Stock Exchange was $16.50. And now they said, "Holy shit, we thought the best we were going to do was nine!"

One night early on in my time at Willis I was back home in New Jersey, having dinner at a diner in Plainfield, when I had an idea. You watch a ball game or you drive around New York or you go to any Fourth of July picnic in Nebraska or Iowa or Texas or South Carolina and you always see the US flag. Three cheers for the red, white, and blue! Our flag unites us. It inspires us. It reminds us who we are. So I sat down at that diner in Plainfield, New Jersey, and sketched out a rough design of a Willis flag on the back of a napkin. Believe me, I'm no artist. It was a crude sketch. But I gave it to our head of events at Willis, Kathryn Collins, and she did a great job designing the pins, which I then asked everyone at Willis to wear.

My thinking was that there are so many fiefdoms, I needed to work to establish the mentality that we were all one team, all united, all *very* united. Just like the British Royal Marines fly their colors, we at Willis were going to do that too. I talked all the time about how Willis is a team sport. None of us is as good as all of us. I was relentless, and sometimes they made fun of me. No, they made fun of me a *lot* for my Joe-isms. But they became part of the culture. People talked about these Joe-isms all the time. They talked about *None of us is as good as all of us*, and they talked about *You can't high-five yourself*—that was another one of my Joe-isms. I used to ask them to imagine someone scoring a touchdown or a goal in soccer and, instead of high-fiving their teammates, high-five themselves. I would have them high-five themselves by slapping their hands together up above their heads. They all felt silly doing it. Of course they did. And I'd say, "How stupid is that? And that's how stupid it is when you have a company where people aren't working together!" Then I'd ask them to high-five the person to their left and say, "Now which felt better? High-fiving yourself? Or high-fiving each other?"

No one had told me the Brits did not wear pins. I found out later that it just wasn't their thing, like they didn't wear baseball caps. They didn't dive into conversation with strangers the way we Americans like to do, and they didn't wear pins. But I didn't know that when I had all these pins made and got the word out that we expected everyone to wear them. The move was not a popular one. Everyone resented it, some more than others. Some complained about it, though usually out of earshot of me. Most of them did their best not to wear them but at the same time tried hard not to get into hot water because of that. It led to all sorts of comic antics, like people seeing me in the hallways of the Willis offices and holding their hands to cover the spot on their lapel where they did not have a pin.

"What's wrong?" I'd needle them with a smile. "What's wrong with your hand?"

People would duck into doorways when they saw me because they didn't have their pin on. It got to be hilarious. And I would never say anything about the pin. I would simply stare at their lapel and let them come up with their own reaction.

"Ah, Mr. Chairman, I'm sorry I don't have my pin on," one clever fellow told me. "I left it on my pajamas."

You build culture that way. The "pajamas" story got around and became part of the folklore. None of this had to do with business. It all had to do with things you do to stimulate peoples' spirits and stimulate their heads and their hearts, and all of a sudden you're building a culture. I didn't know so many people would be so against being asked to wear pins, but as it turned out, that suited my wishes just fine. I wanted to unite people, and I did a great job of that: they were united in their universal dislike of being asked to adopt a Yankee tradition like wearing pins. They were very united.

I made so many missteps and mistakes, I have to laugh at myself looking back—so many things that I would never have tried if I knew then what I know now. But that's the point: I didn't. To lead, to change a culture, you've got to take action, you've got to let it fly and accept that you're going to get it wrong a good amount of the time. Most people come in to change the culture and so they replace the people. I didn't do that. I stuck with the same people because I was the one who was the outsider, so I thought changing the people was a mistake. Before me, they never held big meetings of all five thousand of the Willis employees based in London, but I brought everyone together in a big theater shortly after I started in the new job for one big meeting. I spoke for two or three hours and had them excited. I talked about how I was going to make sure that, on my watch, we got a gleaming new Willis headquarters building constructed—and that earned a big ovation.

Every leader who inspires people and fires them up will also turn some people off. If you convince people they need to change their ways for a good reason, they'll be with you. They'll be with the program. But people naturally resist change. They get their backs up if you ask for them to give too much. I was so enthusiastic, so positive, and I inspired people, but my high energy level also grated on some people. I would call people on weekends. I would call people when they were on vacation. I myself never minded being called on weekends. I never minded being called when I was on vacation. I'm a workaholic. I love to work. But some of the people I was calling were not comfortable with having their weekends or vacations interrupted with a work call. That led to an anxiety for some of them. That led to resentment and even some bitterness. As I look back I realize I was wrong. Give people a break sometimes. Let them relax. Let them enjoy a sense of a job well done. I've learned from that mistake. Not everybody was going to be as zealous as I was. Not everybody wanted to work all hours and on weekends and vacations. As a matter of fact, I'm trying not to do that myself these days. I'm trying . . .

It took me years to accept that it wasn't enough to have the best of intentions; I also had to learn when to back off a little. That was a lesson it took me a long, long time to take to heart, but eventually I did, though I'm still working on it. That's something anyone reading this book should keep in mind as well: it's great to inspire people, nothing is better, but to each and every action there is an equal and opposite reaction. Call it the physics of leadership: if you set something new in motion, there is going to be a simultaneous counter-reaction, and you can't be surprised or caught off guard by that. You have to accept that. You have to accept dissenters. You have to accept resisters. You have to accept wiseasses who make sarcastic jokes about everything you try to do, even if it's good for them and all their coworkers.

Leading up to a quarterly meeting I would have everyone in a state. They all knew I was going to ask everyone a lot of very detailed questions about every aspect of their area of responsibility. That was less about inspiring people than it was about getting them to know the business inside and out. God is in the details. To me that was just what you did. But for a lot of them it was grueling and scary going through that. It was simple to me: hard work leads to good results. But I didn't want to sacrifice morale. I didn't want people to be fearful and irritable and resentful because they had to go through that grueling questioning. You want a healthy edge of fear, but just a hint of it, like the vermouth in a good martini. You don't want fear to take over. You don't want the respect to go over the line and become out-and-out fear, which in turn makes people feel worried and pent up and hamstrung. That just undercuts and diminishes the inspiration. I always had to balance that. I had to watch that.

For every ten people I inspired, one or two might have been turned off. One or two might have resented the pressure I put on people by raising expectations and asking everyone to be their best. One or two might have been worn down or burned out by a fear of letting me down. That is something any leader needs to be constantly mindful of. It's true I drove some people away. I did have a high turnover, which I'll admit partly had to do with how hard I would drive people. Later, after I'd left Willis, I flew back to London for a hilarious roast where Steve Hearn, deputy CEO of Willis, made sport of me and had everyone laughing talking about my time at Willis. Steve said,

It wasn't easy. We know the reception [you were given]. The parallels between a General Eisenhower and Field Marshall Montgomery are plain to see for all. But just as Ike disarmed his hosts by his homespun smile, so too did Joe by his Trentonian embrace and his characteristic "How ya doin'?"

From the very start Joe knitted the disparate parts of Willis together, a new alliance sixty years later—the UK, Europe, North America, Latin America, Asia, reinsurance, our specialisms—and gave our competitors no quarter. He knew how hard it would be in part because he has always been such a keen student of history, especially that of this nation and our legendary resilience. He knew Churchill had said, "It is not enough that we do our best; sometimes we must do what is *required*." Who in this room has not heard this from Joe in some form or fashion over the past twelve years? And who has not responded with the very best, with what was *required*?

Churchill said, "I have nothing to offer but blood, toil, tears, and sweat."

Those who have talked to Joe face to face, in the Polycom or on the phone, from Monday morning to, yes, Sunday night have felt the force of his blood, toil, tears, and sweat. Some of us are still here to talk about it. I should at this point pause briefly and remember those who have fallen in battle. Those of you with emotion may wish to bow your heads

in remembrance as I call out the list of some of the
fallen soldiers—this may take a minute or two . . .
there are a few of them.

And then the names scrolled on the big screen. He
had me nailed. I was laughing and crying at the same
time.

The years of hard work at Willis culminated in our
plans to open a brand new Willis headquarters building in the city of London, right across from Lloyds,
replacing the World War I–era building they'd been in
for decades. Often it seemed we'd never get there, that
it was too daunting a challenge, but finally we got to
the point at which we were counting down the months
until the new building would open. Lord Peter Levine,
chairman of Lloyds, was visiting me in my New York
office, and I told him how excited we were to finally be
opening the new headquarters.

"Who are you going to get to get to dedicate the
new building?" he asked me.

"Me," I said.

"You have to have a proper dedication.

"Well, what's that?" I asked him.

"You need someone very prominent, preferably
from the royal family."

I gave him a blank look.

"Well, I don't know any royalty," I said. "I knew a couple of dukes in the old neighborhood—Duke Milaci, Duke Snyder—but that's about it."

"Let me see what I can do," he said.

So he pulled out his cell phone and made a call.

"Hello, Amanda, is Andrew there?" he said.

Prince Andrew was not in, as it happened. But Lord Levine was obviously close to him and explained the situation to his assistant Amanda, and soon it was all lined up: Prince Andrew himself was going to be dedicating the new building. I was a little nervous about meeting him. Normally I'd have been thrilled—I'm always excited to meet new people—but in this case they'd given me a whole list of things I was supposed to do and not supposed to do when I was in the presence of royalty. High on the list was "Other than shaking hands, do not ever touch a royal." I touch everyone! How was I going to keep from doing that? The list also scolded me in advance for addressing him as anything other than "Your Royal Highness."

I didn't need to worry. Prince Andrew drove himself up in his own Range Rover, unescorted, and turned out to be warm and fun and down to earth. As soon as I saw that he and I were going to connect just fine, I apologized in advance if I got too friendly and hugged him or otherwise violated protocol.

"That's just who I am," I told the prince.

"Quite all right, quite all right," he told me.

So I gave a speech for the occasion and read from an imaginary letter from my mother that went on about how "My son Joey is really happy that you came to help dedicate the new building" and "Joey is a nice boy, but he's a little nervous because he's never been around royalty, so I hope you'll all be nice to him." Afterward Prince Andrew came up to me with a big smile and told me how much he'd enjoyed the speech, and we clasped our arms together. That was as close as a hug as you're ever going to get from a member of the British royal family. It was a great example of how even what are considered from a distance to be starchy people can turn out to be anything but as soon as you meet them and open your heart to them and take them on their own terms.

People everywhere want to be inspired. We all want the same things. It takes some time and effort sometimes to break through the distractions of differences from country to country. People might look different and dress differently; they might eat different food and wear different clothes, but does any of that really matter? Our hearts are the same everywhere. That, in the end, was a lesson of September 11 I wish we could all have learned, and it's a lesson I was happy to bring home from my great years working in London for Willis. Thanks for inspiring me! So many of you became good friends over my twelve years with Willis, and you might have different ways of showing your emotion sometimes, but you are passionate people with heart. You taught me a lot.

My speeches were no different in England from what they were in the United States. I didn't get any different laughs in England from what I got in the United States, and my stories didn't change. They were all the same. What I found was that by being true to my heart and being true to myself people responded in the same way. If you're authentic and you give your heart, they will give it back. They might take a while, but eventually you see it. I learned the same lesson in other countries again and again. I went to Germany, and everyone told me the Germans have no sense of humor and they're too stiff to warm up to a guy like me. I figured I'd just let it fly and be myself anyway, and even my translator was cracking up. She was revved up, trying to convey my energy and passion. I had a room full of Germans belly laughing and grinning. They just wanted someone to treat them warmly and with heart. They just wanted to be inspired.

From Africa to Asia, Europe to South America, everywhere I've been it's the same story. I gave the first speech to the Chinese Brokers Association at the Peace Hotel in Shanghai, and they gave me this long-stemmed red rose with an extra-long green stem that came up to my neck. My interpreter was standing next to me and was trying to emulate everything I did. As I was speaking, I'd flick at the stem of the rose poking against my neck, which was getting itchy. Sure enough, the interpreter started making the same gesture, flicking at his neck, and he didn't have a rose on. I had to work not to crack up over that. I went to the Netherlands and they gave me a baseball jersey with "Plumeri" on it, then I went to Argentina and they gave me a "Plumeri" soccer jersey. If we are just ourselves, then we're all connected—not through the Internet but through our hearts. We look at people we don't know well, and our first impressions can be so misleading. But that's all just superficial. If you get to know them, the way I got to know so many good people during my years at Willis, I found out they were committed and passionate and full of life and personality; they were good, family-loving people you could talk to the way you'd talk to anyone. Give people the benefit of the doubt, look for the best in them, the humanity in them that unites us all, and you can always inspire them, which is what they all want. We all have hearts—you just have to find them. Once you do that, once you've inspired and excited them, you can take them to new places. You can help them to find new energy and new capability.

Show the Way to Grandma's House

My father instilled in me at a young age that you should always be full of hope and optimism but that hope wasn't enough. Dreams alone didn't count for anything. You also needed to articulate a vision that could then carry you forward to fulfilling those hopes and dreams. Hollywood was known as a dream factory: they encouraged people to take a fantasy and dwell on it—I want to be rich! Or, I want to be a major league ball player! Or, I want to be a movie star! That was nice enough for getting people to go to the picture show, but if a yearning like that stayed in the category of hopes and dreams, then it never progressed to the stage of becoming a clear vision. There's no checking account called the "hope" account. Without a detailed plan, nothing would ever happen for you, and to make that plan work you needed to be able to bring your vision alive in an exciting, understandable way that could fire other people up and energize them to help you turn your hopes and dreams into reality. I like to call this "showing the way to Grandma's house." Like if you took a drive to Grandma's house with the kids and wanted them to settle down after they started getting restless two-thirds of the way there, you got their attention by telling them all about the delicious chocolate-chip cookies Grandma had baked for them, the best cookies you've ever tasted in your whole life, and about all the other treats she was going to have ready. That would get their attention. They'd be picturing those cookies and cakes and smiling at the thought, and you'd have them on board and invested for the long haul of that drive. The same basic dynamic, equipping them to endure the trip, applies in countless other contexts.

Most of what I know about life I learned from my father while growing up in the 1950s. We were a working-class Italian American family in North Trenton, New Jersey, surrounded by working-class families of all backgrounds. There were Polish Americans just a few blocks away, with their churches and their bakeries and their meeting halls and, one block over, a street that was mostly African American. Around the corner was Rossi's family bakery, where I would get cannoli every weekend and bread every morning, and near that was the grocery store run by Mrs. Sollami, the mother of my Little League coach. We all got along because we had to get along, all of us looking for ways to find a better future.

My father was my best friend. He loved life and loved people and went through his days looking for ways to make everyone he saw feel good. He took all the qualities his own father had in abundance and added to them. He had an amazing faith that good things could always happen, and he passed that on to us every day in ways large and small, especially every Sunday, when family tradition called for us all to get lessons in passion, in dreaming, and in believing. Every Sunday in the 1950s we would go to church as a family and then come home for a big pasta meal. Then we would get in the car and go for a ride so my father could inspire us by showing us big, beautiful, awe-inspiring houses that to him represented the American Dream.

"If you go to school and you work hard, you can have a house like that," my father would tell us while we stared out the car window at one amazing house after another. Then we would stop for ice cream at Dairy Queen.

We did the same thing every Sunday like clockwork, the same church, the same pasta meal, the same houses, and the same words from our father. It was like an incantation, the way he repeated the words, *You can have a house like that.* That was how my brothers and I were raised. How could you have that experience and *not* grow up to be a dreamer? How could you not wind up with a positive view on life when that was the message you heard every Sunday? It wasn't that my father saw a big house or being rich as the be all and end all of existence. Not at all. He just wanted us to believe in possibility. He wanted it instilled deep inside us that if we put our heart and soul into working for what we wanted and into becoming the best we could be in our chosen field, then anything was possible.

My youngest brother, Paul, got the message, though it took him in a direction very different from mine. He ended up as a great guitarist, one of the top blues guitarists in the country, and he still is today. If you go to YouTube, you can find him ripping up "T-Bone Shuffle" on his Fender Stratocaster. My middle brother, Sam, took another direction. He served as a cop for thirty-five years and was elected sheriff, with wide margins, of Mercer County a number of times. He was and is a very popular member of his community. He built up a renowned career in law enforcement and was head of the police force of the Port Authority of New York and New Jersey, giving him jurisdiction over the World

Trade Center and other major shared facilities of the two states. Over the years he has played a prominent role in thwarting countless terrorists.

Three brothers. Three dreams. Three visions. We have all been able to do a lot in life because in some way we were all still living out the vision instilled in us during those car rides with my father. The vision just manifested for each of us in different ways.

Growing up I loved sports and always felt like I had my father behind me every time I took the field, whether I was playing for coach Paul Sollami in the North Trenton Little League or for Puggy Malone at Trenton Catholic Boys High School. My father was there energizing me, firing me up. Every single game I had, whether it was baseball or football, he'd always be there in the stands, cheering me on.

"Run hard!" he would yell out.

That was all he said, because he didn't need to say more. His meaning was clear: "Run hard" was his way of saying: *Hustle!* It was his way of saying, *Play with passion! Play with your heart! Play with everything you've got!*

I wasn't the biggest guy on the team, not by a long shot, but I might have had the most heart. Our football coach at Trenton Catholic High was not always a big fan of my abilities, and it's true I wasn't the best player, not by a long shot, but I found a way to contribute. The biggest game of the season, against our archrivals, Trenton High, I scored two touchdowns and caught a pass in the end zone for one of them. It was a great day, and I could hear my father the whole time. I attended Bordentown Military Institute for one year and played all three sports; I played football there with Floyd Little, the future Hall of Famer, and I showed enough potential that I was recruited to come play at the College of William and Mary. Without football I never would have gotten into William and Mary.

I missed hearing my father always there to cheer me on when I moved on to William and Mary, where I played on both the baseball and football teams. My father came to some of our games, but I could hardly expect him to come to all of them; it was too far for him to drive. What was he going to do? Jump on the nearest cloud? I remember a baseball game we played against the Citadel in Charleston, South Carolina. For a Jersey kid like me, this place was a whole different world. It was weird even being there, but interesting. I was just trying to get my bearings at the start of the game when I dug into the batter's box to lead off and start the game. My father always taught me that if you had a fastball pitcher, you stood back in the batter's box to give yourself an extra instant of time, and if you had a junk ball pitcher, you moved as far up in the box as you could to get to the ball before it breaks and then, by definition, it's a hanging curve. I was digging my spikes into the batter's box when all of a sudden I had the strangest sensation. I was just sure I could hear my father's voice urging me to "Run hard!" from somewhere high up above.

I tried to ignore it, but there it was again, what sounded like my father's voice. I looked up and there he was, his smiling face staring back at me from the stands.

"Run hard!" he yelled again.

I could only grin—and play my ass off. That was passion! It turned out my father had his heart set on making this game no matter what. He was able to find a guy who ran a deli to fly him down to the game in a little Piper Cub airplane, only the guy had no idea where he was going. He had never flown that far and knew nothing about navigation. My father told him, "Follow the railroad tracks from Trenton down to South Carolina. We'll be fine." The guy had no instruments, no nothing, but he made it. He got my father there to see me play and cheer me on. That, my friends, is passion!

Like most everyone during those times, my father had some trouble making ends meet. At one point he invested in a shopping mall that was a forerunner of the outlets that would later become such a major trend; this was in 1961, so he was way ahead of his time with the idea, but he had partners on the deal who stole from him, and the whole thing went belly up. He could easily have declared bankruptcy and made things a lot easier on himself, but he refused to do that. He wouldn't go bankrupt.

"People trusted me," he said. "They gave me money based on my name and reputation. I intend to pay them all back." And he gave every one of them what he could so they were all satisfied.

For him that was natural because he was always sure things were going to take a turn for the better.

It didn't take much for my father to break out in song, especially uplifting tunes like his favorite, "Pennies from Heaven." It just might be the most optimistic song ever written, and that was my father: *look at the positive side of things.* As kids we took it for granted—that was just our father's thing. We smiled, we enjoyed it, but we didn't think too much about it. But when you get older and think about the words to the song, it really hits you hard—what an upbeat, positive song. What a statement on how my father saw life. I love the song too. In fact, if you ask real nice, I might come out and sing it for you. If hearing that song doesn't make you feel good, I don't know what will. Look at whatever is bothering you and think about it from the bright side: it's not rain; it's pennies from heaven raining down on you.

My father's optimism rubbed off on me. It shaped me when I was young and stayed with me. I finished up at William and Mary and was ready to run out and grab my future. "Run hard" held true off the sports field too. I got married a week after graduation in 1966. For two years I taught and coached baseball and football at Neshaminy High School in Langhorne, Pennsylvania, and had a great time doing it too, but I had bigger plans for myself and my future. I decided to quit and go to law school, but first I joined the Army Reserve. I went down to boot camp in Fort Jackson, South Carolina, and plans for my future had nothing to do with what drove me to excel there—it was pure survival instinct. I was scared to death the whole time, thinking about my wife being pregnant and my need to provide for her and the baby. I did everything I could to excel. I was so scared that I ran so hard, and I ended up as the top trainee of my cycle, chosen out of more than one thousand recruits to receive a medal from the general. That was in October of 1968, the same month as the Mexico City Summer Olympics and a few weeks before President Richard Nixon was elected president.

I got accepted to New York Law School and registered, and as it turned out, my last class ended at noon, which meant I could go out and look for a job in the afternoon. I figured I'd go work at a Wall Street law firm doing whatever they wanted me to do. I needed the money, and I thought it would be a great way to absorb a practical sense of what lawyers really did. I knew even at that age that I was always going to be a guy who learned from watching people at least as well as I learned from putting my nose in a book. I figured I would try my chances walking door to door, dropping in on law firms and asking for a job. It was kind of fun, rolling the dice without knowing what to expect. I was walking up Broad Street looking at the directories, and any time I saw a firm with three names, that meant it was a law firm. Everybody knows law firms always have three names, right?

At 55 Broad Street I saw a sign for Carter, Berlind & Weill and thought that sounded impressive.

"What can I do for you?" the receptionist asked me, giving me one of those looks receptionists give you to try to make you disappear. But it was going to take a lot more than that to get rid of me.

"Who could I see about a job?" I asked her.

She flashed me a look as if she'd eaten some bad oysters for lunch.

"Well, it's a very small company," she said. "Let me check."

She talked into the phone in a low, conspiratorial voice, nodding now and then, and finally looked back up at me. "Go down the hall, make a left, and ask for Mr. Weill," she said, and I think I saw her smile as I thanked her and walked off in pursuit of this Mr. Weill. I took a left, as instructed, and found a room where a bunch of guys in shirts and ties were running around looking very busy and very focused. One of them turned to face me.

"Are you Mr. Weill?" I asked him.

"Yes, what can I do for you?"

So I sat down and launched into my spiel. And what a spiel it was too. I'd worked it all out ahead of time. I explained how I was going to law school in the morning, learning the academics, but wanted to learn the practical part of the law in the afternoon. I could combine the two and really learn something. Then I could start my meteoric rise to the top. Those were the exact words I used, "meteoric rise to the top." I'll never forget it: I was a kid, giving him a shtick, and he heard me out, his eyes alert but his face blank, giving me no idea what he was thinking.

"I think it's a great idea," he told me when I finally had to pause and come up for air. "But what makes you think you can do that here?"

I thought I had him.

"Well, this is a law firm," I said, smiling.

"No," he said. "This is a *brokerage* firm."

I slid down in my leather chair, slinking as low as I could. I'm not a person who gets embarrassed very often, but at this moment my ears were burning; I felt so foolish. I'd made a hell of a mistake.

"Excuse me, I'm sorry," I said, trying to slide up out of my slippery leather chair.

"No, don't go," Sandy Weill told me.

I was confused, but I slowed down in my attempt to get the hell out of there.

"I think you've got a lot of moxie," Sandy told me. "Tell you what. I'll give you a job in the afternoon after your law school classes. We'll find some things for you to do."

This was Wall Street, 1968, a Brave New World of possibility. I got one taste of the raw energy of the place, the intense, focused decision making and problem solving, all against a backdrop of fancy suits and fortunes to be made, and I loved everything about it. I was the kid in the office to whom they gave jobs no one else wanted to do, working from a desk shoved halfway into a closet, with the other half hanging out into the hallway. Sometimes I'd be buying furniture or getting coffee. Other times I'd fix an operations problem or write an employee benefits program because it was such a small operation. I had to do some tedious tasks, but I didn't care.

Those days have stayed with me and made me who I am. Back then I was the kid in the office, and people would literally tap me on the back of the head playfully, the way you do with a kid, and call me "Joey, baby!" I loved that sense of camaraderie. They liked having me around because my enthusiasm and excitement about every day of work there rubbed off on people, everyone from the receptionist to Sandy Weill himself. They smiled to see me trying so hard, and they gave me challenging work because they liked my attitude and work ethic. It ended up being the best education I could ever have gotten.

Today I keep that same attitude with my own employees. It's the key to getting us through the boring or difficult things along the way to what we really want. "Tell me about Grandma's house!" I'll say to someone in the lunch room or in the elevator. After the initial head scratching from the uninitiated, they catch on to what I'm really asking: "What is your *vision* of where we are going? What is your *passion*?" Before long they're talking openly and excitedly about the future—*their* future—and getting fired up about the possibilities. It's a feeling I'm always thrilled to pass on and see take root in others, and it wouldn't have been possible if I hadn't grown up with a dad who shared so much passion for taking chances, seeing good things ahead with vision and clarity, and insisting on a terrific future. He taught me that you always need to stay focused and optimistic on your way to Grandma's house, even if you don't know where that road might take you along the way.

"Tell me about Grandma's house!" I'll say to someone in the lunch room or in the elevator. After the initial head scratching from the uninitiated, they catch on to what I'm really asking: "What is your *vision* of where we are going? What is your *passion*?"

When I started as CEO of Willis I thought back to those days and made an announcement that got everyone's attention: when we build our new headquarters building we are going to save the construction guys some work. That's right, we would have no doors on any of the offices in the place except for conference rooms and the like. We wanted everyone who worked there to understand: we believed in communication. We believed in popping your head into someone's office— including the CEO's—to say hello or discuss a point that had just come up.

Every morning I came into the office at Willis it took me fifteen minutes to make it twenty yards down the hallway from the elevator because I was stopping to talk to people, checking in with them to see how they were doing. If you help other people feel good, you're going to feel good too. But it had a deeper importance: if no one talks to each other and people just exchange e-mails and memos, that's a cold corporate culture. There's no emotion there. No heart. To create a workplace where people want to be, where they love what they're doing and want to do it better, the first thing you need to do is open it up and encourage people to talk to each other, no matter what they're feeling.

The next thing you do is to build a sense of shared expectation about the future. You need to communicate your vision in fresh and fun ways that people can understand. You need to communicate the passion that goes together with that vision. For years I've liked to do that by talking to people about Grandma's house. At first their eyes kind of glazed over, but they would be curious, so I would start asking questions.

"How many of you have got children?" I would ask a group.

Most of them raised their hands.

"Did you ever take a car trip with your kids?" I would ask.

There would be grumbles of assent.

"You're grumbling because you know how long these car trips can be and how rowdy these kids can get in the backseat." I would say. "They lose interest! Every ten miles they ask, 'When are we going to get there?' They start roughhousing with each other. You've got to do something to get them on board. You've got to do something to get these kids to endure the trip, right?"

Everyone would be right there with me.

"So how many of you have ever made up stories so you can get the kids excited and focused on a vision for where they're going so they can settle down and endure the trip?" I ask. "For me that was always talking about 'Grandma's house.' We're going to Grandma's house, I'd tell the kids, and she's going to have cake and ice cream and toys for you, but not unless you settle down first."

If that wasn't enough, for miles of driving I'd go on about the delicious chocolate-chip cookies Grandma had baked special for them and what a treat that was going to be—if they settled down. I always found a way to paint a vision of how great it was going to be when we got to Grandma's house. The words *Grandma's house* took on a resonance of their own. It was like they were magic.

With corporations and all other groups it's the same thing. You've got to paint a vision for where you're going so the employees come to work every day ready to endure the boring or difficult things along the way before you get to the sweet stuff, the payoff after weeks or months or years of work, the thing that makes it all worthwhile. I've called that "Grandma's house" at different companies where I've worked, and it becomes a fun thing for everyone.

"Tell me about Grandma's house!" I'd say to someone in the lunch room or in the office elevator.

I was asking, *What is your* vision *of where we are going? What is your* passion? People loved it and would give me their answers, sometimes short and sweet, sometimes longer and more dramatic, but in every case talking to me about "Grandma's house" fired them up. Openness and passion go hand in hand, from the openness of ripping the doors off the offices of your company to the openness of not trying to hide from being honest and true, in both feeling what you're feeling and expressing it, to the openness of talking about Grandma's house. It all starts with having heart and being yourself.

Cut Your Own Path

I was only six years old in 1950 when my grandfather died of a heart attack. He was just fifty-nine years old and had always been a presence in my life. He told me when I was young that to gain respect you go out there and earn it your own way. You work harder than the next guy, you do your job better than the next guy, and you choose your own destiny, and no one can say nothin' except *Job well done.*

My grandfather always believed in spreading good cheer and making people feel good. He was an upbeat guy. When he died his wake was in the Villalba Club, named for the town back in Sicily where my grandfather and so many others in the neighborhood immigrated from. There were lines of people waiting to go see his body. The ballroom on the second floor of the club was made into a funeral parlor, and mourners lined up along

It was a great day for Trenton when the stars of the greatest baseball team ever, the 1927 New York Yankees, including Babe Ruth (second from left), along with Lou Gehrig, came to town soon after winning the World Series that year. Made possible by my grandfather, Joseph Plumeri (second from right). *NJ Advance media/Landov*

the stairway and out the front door downstairs. That was something! He'd got what he came to America to find: acceptance and respect. And as Jackie Robinson later would, he had done that through baseball.

For generations baseball has been helping immigrants and the unfairly excluded become more integrated into American culture. Looking back at a great national icon like Babe Ruth, it's easy to miss how much of an outsider he had been while growing up because of his immigrant roots. Ruth was the first real baseball star, part of the greatest Yankee teams ever in the 1920s. He was the first one whose popularity overflowed the world of sports and turned him into a full-fledged national celebrity. But if it were not for the escape baseball offered, the rough-neck world of rowdy German immigrants in Baltimore, Maryland, where he grew up and roamed the streets would have claimed him, the way it did his parents. His mother, the daughter of German immigrants, was sickly and died young. His father, the grandson of German immigrants from Prussia and Hannover, was a one-time barkeep who died after a saloon brawl when his head hit a curb.

Ruth's German roots always stayed with him. Even at the peak of his fame, playing for those great New York Yankees teams of the era, hitting sixty home runs in 1927 while wearing the pinstripes, he still spoke

German at times. Yet to kids all over the country, to fans of all ages, the Babe was as American as it got. To my grandfather, an immigrant from Sicily, there was no greater symbol of America and Americana than the Bambino. My grandfather was born July 1, 1890, in Villalba, Sicily, and that fall his father, Salvatore, left his baby son and wife to make the voyage to the United States and settle in North Trenton, New Jersey. So I can say with pride that the Plumeri family arrived in the New World aboard the Victoria on November 21, 1890, when my great-grandfather arrived in New York City. He soon established himself as "one of the pioneers of the Italian community" in Trenton, according to the book *Prominent Families of New Jersey*: "First establishing himself financially, he sent for his wife and children two years after his own arrival, so that they joined him in 1892," the book explains. "Salvatore Plumeri first found work with the John A. Roebling's Sons Company, and he remained with the firm for nineteen years. At the end of that time, in 1909, he went into the retail liquor business and also established a macaroni factory—the first in Trenton for the manufacture of Italian macaroni."

A lot of people from Sicily started coming to Trenton, and the men would form clubs honoring their hometowns, like the Villalba Club, but even with so many Italian immigrants in town, it still wasn't easy for my grandfather growing up. He'd be called wop. He'd be called dago. He couldn't go down the street without someone yelling at him or throwing stones at him or throwing a stick. But that's just how it was then. People forget. Irish were called micks or potato heads. Every immigrant group had to go through that hazing.

From a young age my grandfather worked as hard as he could. He went to public school in Trenton, and then, the same book explains, "When he was fourteen, he quit school for the time being, and took a position at Clark's Lamb Works, putting in twelve hours a day. He continued with this firm for about a year, and then went to work for the New Jersey Tile Company as a general tile worker, remaining with this firm for a few years. He then went with the Star Porcelain Company, and later with the Trenton Porcelain Company." He took night courses at a business college, became president of the Electrical Porcelain Workers Union Local No. 266, and, starting in 1918, got into the real estate business.

My grandfather didn't like being called dago and wop. Of course, he didn't. But he didn't whine or fuss. No, he went out and *earned* respect. He knew what his ticket to acceptance and respect was, and he knew it came wrapped in horsehide with red seams. That's right: baseball. Norman Rockwell didn't paint football—he painted baseball, the sport that was as all-American as apple pie. My grandfather knew that if you were accepted into baseball, that meant you were accepted into society, because baseball and Americana were the same thing.

That was how my grandfather ended up standing outside of Yankee Stadium in October 1927, the final month of the season Babe Ruth became the first man ever to hit sixty homers in a season, the month the Yankees swept the Pittsburgh Pirates in the World Series. Lou Gehrig hit forty-seven that season and had 175 RBIs. That was the year of destiny, the year of Murderers' Row. The Yanks won 110 out of 154 games and were the greatest team ever, pretty much everyone agrees. My grandfather stood outside the Yankee clubhouse waiting with ten hundred-dollar bills to flash at the Babe. He got his attention too.

"What do you got there?" Ruth asked my grandfather.

"This is for you if you'll come and barnstorm," my grandfather told him.

Deal closed. Ruth even talked Gehrig into coming along with him to Wetzel Field in Trenton for the exhibition game that October 11, only three days after the Yankees finished their World Series sweep. This was big news, and the *Trenton Times* trumpeted the coming appearance of the two great Yankees, noting on October 10, "Gehrig and Ruth initially were scheduled for a game in Portland, ME, but the Trenton promoters outbid Portland." That they did! The article described my grandfather as "a business man who has been interested in local baseball." That he was!

A column in the same paper that day by William R. Clark declared, "The high cost of home runs is indicated in the announced price that George Glasco and Joseph Plumeri are guaranteeing Babe Ruth and his companion in crime, Lou Gehrig, to appear in Trenton," but it did not divulge any figure.

Glasco, my grandfather's partner, talked to Cannonball Dick Redding, the player-manager of the team squaring off against the visiting stars. "Now look, you know why all these people are here," Glasco told him, according to John Holway's book *Blackball Stars*. "You know what they came to see. They're out here to see Ruth hit home runs, right?"

"Right."

"Now when the Babe comes to bat, no funny business."

"Got ya. Right down the pike."

Ruth and Gehrig made their way over to Wetzel Field, and the place was so packed that the outfield fences bulged in toward the field. The announced attendance was thirty-five hundred paid, but several thousand local schoolchildren also showed up and kept hopping the fences to run out onto the field. It was a short porch in right field, and for Ruth it was like target practice. He flied out his first two times up, then homered in the sixth inning and again in the seventh, each time prompting the kids in the stands to swarm the field. Both times order was restored and play continued. Then when Ruth came up again in the eighth, he clouted yet another home run, and what looked like every kid in Trenton rushed the field.

"Twice before the eighth inning, as Ruth lifted the ball over the right field wall, hundreds of boys swarmed into the field to romp from third to home with the King of Swat, each time holding up the game for fifteen minutes before the field could be cleared," the next day's *New York Times* reported. "However, after his third homer in the eighth with two on base, officials found it impossible to get the fans from the field and the game was called."

It was one of the greatest days ever in my hometown. All those boys who swarmed the field talked about it their entire lives. Men of my father's generation would always tell me for years to come about that amazing day when Trenton felt to them like the center of the world. Trenton got to be part of the greatest baseball season ever, the '27 Yanks, thanks to my grandfather. He never had to worry again about not being accepted or not being known. Everyone in Trenton knew just who he was and said hello when he walked down the street. He was a man about town. He just had a little agency, real estate and insurance, but everyone loved him.

For five years the New York Giants had a minor league affiliate in Trenton, and my grandfather was a part-owner of the team. I turned seven the last year the Trenton Giants were in town, and I can remember going to Dunn Field to watch them play. I was brought up on baseball the way a jockey's family is brought up on horses or a surfer's family is brought up on waves. I was brought up to enjoy and love baseball. It was in my blood.

"You're going to be a cross between Clarence Darrow, Joe DiMaggio, and Frank Sinatra," my father would tell me often when I was little.

So I started taking singing lessons, and this was a big deal for my family. We weren't poor, but we didn't have a lot of money for extra expenditures. My teacher's name was Lilly Oros, and my mother would give me two dollars for each singing lesson, but before I went for my singing lesson I stopped at the gas station and got two dollars worth of nickels and played the pinball machine, because if I could hit the pinball machine and win big, obviously I'd be set. I could buy all the candy I wanted and still have two bucks left to pay my teacher. If I lost the two dollars, which I invariably did, I'd explain to Miss Oros that my parents would see her later about squaring up our tab.

A year went by, and by then I owed Lilly Oros $104. This might have gone on months longer, but my mother bumped into Lilly Oros on the street.

"You owe me a hundred and four dollars," she said. That was a lot of money at that time.

"Why do we owe you that?" my mother exclaimed.

I've never forgotten the beating I took that night from my father after Lilly Oros explained what I had been doing. I think he hit me twice in my whole life. Once was that night. The other time was when I wrecked the car, a green 1961 Mercury station wagon, when I was sixteen years old driving on a learner's permit. Come to think of it, that might be why to this day green is not my favorite color.

So maybe becoming the next Frank Sinatra was going to be a challenge, but I figured I had the other two in my back pocket. To me the name Darrow meant smart and a fighter, and I decided I'd be a lawyer too. As to Joltin' Joe, to every Italian American kid DiMaggio was our idol. In early 1949 he became the first ballplayer to sign a contract for $100,000 a year. But my American League team growing up was not the Yankees but the Philadelphia A's, those Connie Mack teams that played at Shibe Park. Philadelphia was only about thirty miles away from us, closer than heading up to Ebbets Field in Brooklyn or Yankee Stadium in the Bronx. I could hitchhike in to Philly to see a game at Shibe Park, right down Roosevelt Boulevard from Trenton, and a buck would get me a 50 cent grandstand seat, two hot dogs, and a Coke. Those were the days of the transistor radio, and I would carry the thing around right up next to my ear and always be listening to a ball game.

I was as big a fan as you could get. One of my fondest memories was when the Phillies played the Yankees in the 1950 World Series. My dad managed to get tickets for Game Five. I don't think I'd ever been more excited about anything. The Series started in Philadelphia, and the Yankees won the first game and the second game, both by one run. Again in Game Three up in the Bronx it was a one-run win for the Yankees. Then in Game Four the Bombers won easily—a four-game sweep, and I was out of luck. There was no Game Five! I never got to that World Series. I was so devastated that my father made me a promise: if the World Series was ever in New York or Philadelphia again, we'd go.

He was true to his word too, which worked out great for me in years to come. I remember watching Jackie Robinson play at Ebbets Field against the Yankees in the World Series when I was nine years old. It was a very big racial divide; the Dodgers had African Americans playing for them—Don Newcombe, Roy Campanella, and Jackie. They had a large following from the black community, in those days called the Negro community, and the Yankees were all white with pinstripes and black and white uniforms, with the Brooklyn players making a nice contrast in Dodger blue. It was a clear baseball contrast, but it was an especially stark social contrast. What was interesting was that the Yankees always won. And if you look back on those days, the white guys always won. The Bombers beat the Dodgers in both the 1952 and 1953 World Series, with Jackie setting records for double plays by a second baseman and still very much a presence, and then, in 1955, the Brooklyn Dodgers finally won it all—the Boys of Summer.

I admired Jackie Robinson not only for baseball but also for the way he carried himself and the way he led. Above all I was impressed by his courage. Breaking the color barrier was a bigger social issue than baseball. Jackie Robinson's context for showing his courage and his heart was baseball. If somebody said Jackie Robinson did what he did only because he loved baseball, I'd have a hard time believing that. He wanted to play, he had the ability, and he knew a lot of people after him wanted to have that chance as well, if only somebody with enough talent and courage could get in there and break the traditions of the game. He knew it would be rough, a nightmare for him and his wife, but he expected that over time his skill and intelligence and serious moral purpose would make an impression on people. He was right.

Jackie Robinson showed me that what happened on a baseball field could be as important as anything in life—and, years later, when he worked with a group of committed businessmen to bring baseball back to Trenton, my father showed me the same thing. We had been without minor league baseball for decades. Most people in town had long forgotten the glory days of the Trenton Giants, owned by my grandfather and featuring the likes of Willie Mays, and did not see minor league baseball as fashionable. Put it this way: baseball was the last thing on my mind when I went in to see my father in 1991 soon after he'd had quintuple bypass surgery at age seventy-eight. He was lying there in the bed, looking pale, and I wanted to shake my head.

"I gotta get you a house in Florida," I told my father. "You can go down there and relax."

His eyes came to life.

"Relax?" he said. "I don't want to relax. We need to have a baseball team here in Trenton."

I could see where this was going. Talking my father out of anything once he was set on it was all but impossible. Still I tried. "Pop, think of your heart!" I told him. "How many Plumeri men have died from bad hearts? I want you around."

He didn't hear a word I said. I could almost see the outfield lights of a stadium gleaming in his eyes, the crack of bat on ball ringing in his ears. "Okay, even if it wasn't a crazy idea for you to take this on, what makes you think it's even possible?" I asked him. "This is not a good idea. Where in the hell are you going to get the money to build a baseball stadium? Sixteen to twenty million dollars in a town that's in decay?"

He perked up at that and gave me a Cheshire Cat smile. He knew he had me, even if I didn't have the faintest clue.

"If we find the money and get the stadium built, will you help me?" he asked.

"Sure, Pop," I said. "Sure thing."

I don't think there was ever anybody who had more civic pride in Trenton than my father. He lived and breathed Trenton. He actually ran for office a couple of times and fell short, but he did serve for a time as an appointed city commissioner, and, believe me, he was very proud of that, but it always bugged him that he had not been elected. The cause of Trenton was in a way his life's work, and he knew everybody, absolutely everybody. The state Trenton was in at the time of his quintuple bypass was something he took personally. Like much of the industrial northeast, it had fallen into decay, with no jobs, no money for basic upkeep, a vicious cycle of neglect and obsolescence feeding on itself, more people moving out of the city than were moving in, and who was moving in was worse than what was moving out in terms of poverty and gangs and drugs.

My father believed Trenton was due for a rebirth, a renaissance. He thought he was just the man to lead the revival and that baseball was a perfect vehicle to reinvent the city. I couldn't see any of it. As much faith as I had in my pop's ability to inspire people and make them feel good, I saw zero potential for this idea of his. How could baseball bring people back to Trenton? He had a vision, and he could see very clearly what was possible, but it was as if I were blindfolded. He could see two miles out there, but I couldn't see a foot.

"You'll help me if we get the money?" he repeated.

"Sure, Pop," I said. "Yeah, yeah, yeah."

With that he was off and running. He got out of the hospital and went to work. One day he would be meeting with civic leaders, talking up a return of baseball to Trenton, telling the story one more time of his father bringing the Babe and Gehrig to town back in 1927, the next day he'd be on the radio covering all the same ground again, and then next he'd have gotten himself on TV to reach still more people. I was busy in New York with my work and only half paying attention, but my brother was in Trenton and worked hard on my father's behalf. He went to New Jersey's governor to ask for money. He shook every tree he could find. He believed in our father and backed him when I was doing nothing to help. My brother would call to give me regular updates on their progress, and I'd just shake my head and smile. I couldn't believe it would all add up to anything, but you had to give the old guy credit for going for it.

Really, I should have figured out a lot sooner that my father and his partner were playing a winning hand.

It's not complicated, really: when you have passion and you truly believe in something, you can be very convincing. No one can get rid of you. No one can beat you. If you have that combination of passion and knowing what you're talking about, you're unstoppable. I've often talked about this in companies that I've run. You can beat a team that only has passion because at some point they need to know what in the hell they're doing. You can also beat the team that is capable and accomplished but lacks passion because a time will come when they need to take it up to the next level, but without passion they can't do that; the inspiration is not there. But a team who knows what it's doing *and* has passion, that team cannot be beat. I should have known my father and his partners could not be stopped, but I'd doubted him early and my doubt persisted.

"What do you mean, 'They got it done'?" I asked my brother Sam when he called to give me the news.

"They got it done," Sam said. "They got the county to approve $16.5 million to build the stadium."

I could have whistled out loud. I knew another phone call was coming soon, and sure enough, my father didn't waste much time.

"Jeez, Dad, that's great," I told him. "But take it easy. You've got to worry about your heart."

"You told me if we got the stadium built, you'd help me," he said.

I put him off by telling him he needed to find a team to play in his new stadium, so he went to work on that. Not long after that I got a call from Yankee owner George Steinbrenner one day.

"Are you related to Sam Plumeri?" he asked me.

"Yes, he's my father," I said.

"Tell him to stop harassing me!" Steinbrenner said.

It turned out my father was so intent on getting an affiliation with a major league baseball team that he had been leaving countless messages for Steinbrenner to call him. That wasn't the way to go about getting that done, but he was so passionate that he was trying whatever might work. Can you imagine a man in his late seventies making cold calls?

My father and his partners, Joe Caruso and Jim Maloney, were off to a good start, but they still needed money. For the first season after they had the stadium built, the Trenton Thunder played minor league games there but without having a franchise approved by Major League Baseball. Tony Clark, the future star for the Detroit Tigers, played for Trenton that season. It was a lot of fun. But it was all precarious. Then my father and his partners were called into a meeting with some fellow minor league owners, and the whole thing came to a head.

"We were being grilled," Joe Caruso remembers now. "We had borrowed money when we bought the team, and they were using that as an issue."

I was sitting there in that meeting, listening to the grilling and not knowing what to do. I was thinking of this as a business, a business that could never work, and I was ready to bang my head against the table because I had told my father I would help him, but my business-man brain was telling me *no, no, no.* Finally I told my businessman brain to take a hike. I kept looking at my father, seeing that look in his eyes that reminded me how incredibly important this was to him, and I went with my heart instead. They needed more equity to agree to accept the franchise, and I was going to give it to them.

"I'm part of this, and I'm guaranteeing it!" I told them. "I'll put up my net worth."

I pulled out my financial statement, and that was that. What could they say? I put up everything I had, every dollar I'd worked so hard to earn. It actually turned out to be a great business decision because that team has done very well over the years. But above all it was the right decision because I'd given my father what he deserved and what he'd always wanted: he may not have been elected to office in Trenton, but once I'd pledged my net worth and the team was accepted, he became more than the mayor of Trenton. Everyone knew what he had done for the city, and no one ever forgot it.

"He changed the course of the city," Joe Caruso remembers. "His passion for Trenton kept us all going.

You have to realize one thing: when we were negotiating to bring the team to Trenton, there was only one other minor league baseball teams in New Jersey. The city of Trenton did not have a McDonald's. The city of Trenton was the only capital city in America, including Alaska, that did not have a hotel in the city limits. Office buildings near the stadium were 75 percent vacant. The city of Trenton did not have an arena. It didn't have anything. When we brought minor league baseball back to Trenton, people came back. We gave them a reason to come to Trenton: the Trenton Thunder experience. Those office buildings next to us? They're now 100 percent occupied. The steel foundry building that was empty for twenty years? That's a restaurant now because of us. There's a McDonald's four blocks from the stadium. The city has a Wyndham hotel. None of that was there when we got there."

My father had not changed Trenton's history single-handedly. He'd worked closely with his partners and others got involved, too. As Joe Caruso remembers, *"County Executive Bob Prunetti was very helpful in his stewardship of this game-changing idea to bring baseball back to Trenton and worked closely with the ownership team throughout the process."* But the entire effort was guided by my father's passion for Trenton, his belief in its future. "Sam was the local guy and very much loved in the city," Joe Caruso continued. "He was proactive with the local Chamber of Commerce guys and had a huge impact for us getting traction in the press early in the process. That gave us time to get the story worked out with the county, which we needed."

Soon the city was in full revival. They built up the waterfront next to the new ballpark. Before, there had been a garbage dump and urban blight along the water. Now they had restaurants there. The city built an arena for minor league hockey games and minor league basketball games and major acts like Pavarotti and Earth, Wind and Fire. The Trenton Thunder led the league in attendance and were named national minor league team of the year more than once. In fact, the Thunder was seen nationally as a symbol of the resurgence of minor league baseball in general, as the *New York Times* wrote in a big June 1995 piece. Reporter David Stout wrote in an article that gave me goose bumps,

> Well before the baseball game, the purple sky and the wind-whipped ripples on the Delaware River told of a storm coming. Some of the fans streaming into Waterfront Park to watch the Trenton Thunder play the Binghamton Mets cast anxious glances upward. If a minor league game means less than, say, the cost of living or the fate of the blue whale, it still means a lot to those who fill the Thunder's idyllic playground, where enthusiasm for the summer

game burns as fiercely as the midday sun. . . . After decades of decline, minor league baseball has suddenly become a viable industry—an economic-development tool and a source of pride for downtrodden cities like Trenton, a magnet for commerce in the hinterlands of Sussex County. Nationwide, attendance has more than doubled since 1980—to 33 million in 1994—and demand for franchises has increased 27 percent, according to the National Association of Professional Baseball Leagues, which governs the minor leagues.

Imagine—Trenton, a success story being talked up in the pages of the *New York Times*! He went on to say, "What is truly splendid about games in the year-old ball park next to the river is that they are played with abandon by young men—boys, really—who may still harbor dreams of the big money in the big leagues but have not yet lost their sense of fun. . . . The Thunder is owned by Garden State Baseball Limited Partnership, whose principals include Samuel Plumeri. His father was a part-owner of a minor league team of yesteryear, the Trenton Giants, who had a player thought to have some big league potential. (His name was Willie Mays.) . . . Despite finishing last in the Eastern League's Southern Division in 1994, the Thunder was third in overall attendance. This year, the team has been playing around .500. It leads the league in attendance, having drawn 156,591 fans to its first 29 games."

We had hope in Trenton again. The city was alive. Thanks, Pop. Thanks for what you did for Trenton, but thanks especially for what you did for me. I'd spent all those years hustling to get ahead in the business world and trained myself to make tough decisions about cutting costs, imposing discipline, trimming a bloated work force, inspiring people. Those were useful tools to have. Every good businessman needs to sharpen those blades. But if that's all you are, then you're nothing. My father devoted the last years of his life to helping bring baseball back to Trenton and reviving the whole city, and he did it because he cared. He did it because he had passion and heart. I almost blew it. I almost forgot to stop thinking like a businessman and instead to go ahead and be my father's son. Back when I was a boy sitting next to him at the ballpark I learned how heart and passion had everything to do with baseball. Jackie Robinson and my grandfather showed me that what happened on a baseball field could be as important as anything in life. They showed me that it could be a place to show a deep and inspiring courage, a place to inspire us to be ourselves and follow our own paths.

Principle 4

Let Sadness Teach You

B etty Ford was right. I met President Jerry Ford and
the former First Lady at a work dinner in the early
1980s not long after my son Chris had begun to have
problems with anorexia. Betty was a very gracious
listener. She'd turned her own addiction issues into a
remarkable positive, founding the renowned Betty Ford
Center, which has helped many thousands of people.
She had real insight into what it takes for people to get
back on track.

"Joe, your son's problems go back to a lack of
self-esteem," Betty told me. "Anorexia and self-esteem
go together in the same way that drug problems and
self-esteem go together."

Those words stayed with me, and so did both Fords'
warmth and sympathy in listening to me talk about
Chris. Then a few days later I was in for a surprise.

The day my son Chris graduated from the prestigious Culinary Institute of America as a trained chef was one of the happiest of my life. I believed the issues Chris grappled with throughout his life, all because I wasn't there enough for him when he was growing up, were finally behind us. How wrong I was. *Image courtesy of Joe Plumeri*

"President Ford sent me a letter," Chris told me.

I couldn't believe it! I hadn't even given the Fords an address for Chris. The former president of the United States had taken the time and initiative to look it up on his own. This is what Ford had written to my son: "I just had dinner with your father, and he loves you very much. All families have problems. It's very important that you work together as a family, and everything will be okay."

If only, if only. Yes, all families have problems, and it takes honesty, sometimes painful honesty, for us to try to solve those problems—or to learn from them. I can't write a book about the importance of being your-self, about being passionate and having heart, if I don't delve into the story of losing my son Chris. You can't hide from the truth of your life and call that being your-self. "Being yourself" sounds like the easiest thing in the world, and in a way it is, but it can be hard too. It can be challenging. In the same way we neglect others because we are too busy, too caught up in the challenge of the moment, we neglect ourselves. We neglect an honest dialogue with ourselves about how we're han-dling the most important challenges in our lives, like doing our best to be there for the ones we love. That is how we can be ourselves. I wish I'd done a better job of that as a father and that I didn't need to go through the story now to offer my own life as a cautionary tale. But it's the only honest way. It's the only way to show how much I believe in what I'm urging you to adopt as your own approach to life.

Betty Ford was right that Chris's problem stemmed from low self-esteem. Something was missing. Something was off. I can see that now, looking back, but there was nothing at all wrong with the kid when he was little. He was always a sweet, sensitive kid, full of life and quick with a smile. He was a good athlete and an okay student. In short he had all the ingredients to be successful. All he needed to develop and grow was a father—and he didn't have one. Not really. I didn't raise him. I didn't pay enough attention. I was too self-absorbed to be around enough and present enough for him during his formative years.

I put myself and my own ambitions before him. I was kept away by this business trip or that business trip, this twelve-hour workday or that twelve-hour workday. But even when I was home I wasn't present in the way I should have been. His mother, Nancy, did her best, but too often I wasn't there to do my part. I was worrying about my own career rather than the things that I obviously should have been worrying about. I was preoccupied. My heart was into *me* more than it was into him. That's just a fact. That was where I focused most of my time and effort.

I never sat down with Chris and helped him do his homework. Nor did I help his younger brother Jay or their sister Leslie. I can't remember changing a diaper. Not a single one. Did I read to my kids? I read aloud to my daughter a couple of times, but never to Chris. Like a lot of men of my generation, I looked to my own father as a role model when it came to what a parent should be like. My mother cooked for us and served us our meals and took care of everything domestic, just as you'd expect from a Sicilian mother. My father was working or was a man about town. However, ideas about fatherhood have changed dramatically since then. Fathers still get up and go to work, but they're also expected to change diapers and play with the kids and read to them at night before they go to bed. Today's woman gets today's man much more involved in what goes on in the house. That's a good thing. I left the burden of raising our three kids on Nancy.

I was in the army when Nancy and I got the news that she was pregnant with our firstborn. I kept thinking about how excited I was to be bringing a son into the world and how I wanted everything to be right for him. Then it came time for Chris to be born, and he didn't want to come out. I'm serious: the kid didn't want to come out. Labor had to be induced. His birth was difficult, and his whole life was a struggle as well.

Anorexia became an issue when Chris was thirteen. At first it was hard to know what to think as Chris began to eat less and less. Nancy and I were worried but agreed we'd just have to keep an eye on Chris and hope for the best. Some weeks he'd seem to eat a healthy amount. Other weeks he'd insist on eating by himself in his room, so we didn't know whether he was taking in any nourishment at all. He got thinner and thinner. We worried more and more. Finally we knew for sure we had a problem on our hands, and the question became what to do about it. Chris was wasting away. Eventually he got down to eighty-nine pounds and his toes turned purple. That forced us to make the wrenching decision to send Chris to Fair Oaks Hospital, a treatment facility in Summit, New Jersey, where one of Robert F. Kennedy's sons had gone for drug addiction and gotten clean.

It went the opposite way for Chris. His time at Fair Oaks turned him into a drug addict because the kids at Fair Oaks were almost all drug addicts, not anorexics. We would go in every week for conferences, and Chris never seemed to be getting any better. That didn't seem to matter to the counselors at Fair Oaks. Then one week they told us they were going to let Chris go home ahead of schedule.

"How could you let him go?" I complained. "He's not well."

"Well, we don't want you to keep him here until you run out of insurance," I was told. "We want to let him go so you still have insurance left in case he needs to come back."

I went berserk!

"You're going to measure my son's condition as to whether he's well enough based upon how much insurance I have?" I yelled. "That's crazy. Don't worry about the payment. You just keep him here as long as he needs to be here."

Maybe I should have been eager to get him home. He never did make any progress there. The actress Mackenzie Phillips (from the sitcom *One Day at a Time*) went to Fair Oaks for drug treatment and was encouraged to drink. "Here's my favorite part: for some reason the well-intentioned doctors at Fair Oaks Hospital decided that it was perfectly fine for us drug addicts to continue to drink alcohol," she wrote in her book *High on Arrival*. "Because alcohol wasn't our drug of choice. Well, that was handy."

Chris bounced from one school to another. I dropped him off in the morning at a new school in Connecticut and caught a flight that afternoon to go give a speech in Lake Tahoe. By the time I arrived in California Chris had already gotten thrown out of that school. Within four hours of arriving he'd been expelled for dealing drugs in the town. Four hours!

We couldn't stick him on Alcatraz, but we came up with the next best thing: Secret Harbor, a tough school on Fidalgo Island off the coast of Washington state, in the town of Anacortes, which you had to reach by boat.

All the psychologists there had beards and were strong and tough, the kind who would knock you around if you looked at them wrong. They were so serious that they made you agree to a minimum of eighteen months. Otherwise, they argued, no real healing or growth could take place. He'd been there less than a year when I got a phone call with the news they wanted to let Chris out of the place early.

"You told me it would take eighteen months!" I told them.

"It's remarkable how this kid has recovered," I was told.

Some drug addicts have an ability to manipulate people that is just off the charts. They are gifted performers, able to tell stories or play a part in order to get whatever they want. I knew this was happening. But what could I do? I went out there and picked him up. Almost as soon as we were together Chris and I started arguing about his long, unruly hair. We were at a Seattle hotel for a big meeting of Shearson sales people, and I wanted Chris to get a haircut, so I made him go to the barber in the hotel for a trim.

Now I ask: How come I couldn't take a step away from my day-to-day life at Shearson and slow down and focus on Chris? I could have been asking him how he was doing, what really went on inside the place, how he felt about life, and how he felt about himself. That was one of many opportunities I missed to talk to my kid. You only get so many. And I was arguing with him about his hair?

Chris was a very sensitive kid. Even later, if he got mad, he'd usually cry too because it bugged him so much to be mad. If you showed him love, if you were there for him, he responded. He was great fun to be around, a good friend to his friends, and, as the oldest brother, he was very caring and always there for his sister, looking after her. The kid was full of heart and eager to please, but when you disappointed him the hurt preyed on him and left him confused and directionless. He was always looking for something to fill the void but never finding it. Nothing could work for long because what he really wanted was the basic love and support that I failed to give him when he was a boy.

By high school he was trying to build up his muscles to make up for the hollow feeling inside. He hit the weights the way other kids would binge on video games, but he had no interest in organized sports. I latched on to the idea that playing football would help give him direction. Or maybe I was just looking back on my own time in high school, when I scored two touchdowns in the big game. Maybe I wanted Chris to live his life the way I had mine, or maybe I was hoping to relive my past glory vicariously. I don't know. I just know I ended up negotiating with my son.

"If you maintain a B average and make the football team, I'll get you the Corvette," I told him. "You don't have to start. Just go to practice every day, and you'll get your 'Vette."

So what did Chris do? He got into it. They started him at nose tackle, and when I went to watch his first game he made five unassisted tackles. The kid was a brute. He was a stud!

"God, finally," I said to myself.

I let myself hope. I let myself believe. But it was all an act. Chris didn't care about football. He kept his grades up enough to fulfill our deal, and he started at nose tackle all through his senior year. I truly thought he might play some college ball. But that was the farthest thing from his mind. He got his car, and the transaction was over. He got into Farleigh Dickinson University in Madison, New Jersey, but he was done with football. He was done with trying. He didn't pay any attention and, before long, flunked out. All he'd cared about was that Corvette.

Next Chris decided he wanted to have his own gym, and, stupid me, I invested in a gym. Now, to be clear, this was not some nice fitness center that he could have turned into a success with a variety of people popping in after work to ride the Lifecycle or walk on the tread-mill. No, this was just a smelly room for pumping iron. This was a bunch of guys with bulging necks looking like they came straight off the set of *Jersey Shore*. I put eight thousand dollars into that damn gym, but Chris didn't work at making it a success, and I didn't give him much help. We'd made another deal, one that could never lead to anything but disappointment. He never could focus on anything for very long. Finally we gave in to the inevitable and closed the gym down.

The next thing I knew there were federal agents looking for Chris. He had been passing illegal credit cards for the mob. But the feds were after bigger fish—they wanted him to squeal.

"Why don't you tell them what they need to know?" I asked him.

"I can't do it," Chris told me. "You'd be in danger."

Because Chris would not cooperate, he went to jail. They sent him to a federal correctional institution in Danbury, Connecticut, where he ended up doing eigh-teen months. I finally woke up and realized my son needed me to be his father. I vowed that from that point on I was going to do everything I could. I decided I would visit Chris every single weekend he was incar-cerated to show him how much I loved him, and I did. I didn't miss a weekend. No matter where I might be on business that week, I'd find a way to fly back home for my weekend visit to Chris. I'd drive a few hours up from our house in Scotch Plains, New Jersey, and he always looked happy to see me. He'd be in an orange jumpsuit and would give me a big hug and kiss. We'd chat about life in general or what was going on with him. But it was never more than just scratching the surface. Chris never talked about what he had done to get there.

I'd be cheerful and upbeat when I was with Chris, but then when I got behind the wheel for the three-hour drive back home, left to my own thoughts and feelings, it was always the same: I would be crying as I drove. I almost had myself believing that by being so committed to being there to visit Chris week after week after week in prison I was finally convincing him of something he had never really believed—that his dad loved him. There were moments when I was sure we were making progress, and I was there to celebrate his release with him. I was up before dawn and there in Danbury at seven o'clock in the morning to pick him up. He was a free man again.

"How do you feel?" I asked Chris over breakfast.

"I feel great," he told me.

"So what now?" I asked him.

He paused. I think he was worried about how I would react.

"I want to be a chef," he told me.

This was not a total shock to me. He'd been doing some cooking on the inside and told me on my weekly visits how much he enjoyed that. I wished he would be a little more realistic, but I also wanted to support and encourage him. At least he was thinking about his future.

"How you gonna be a chef?" I asked, and not in an unfriendly way.

"I thought I might try chef school," he said.

That was how we ended up two hours north of New York City in Hyde Park for a preliminary visit to the Culinary Institute of America. I figured we might as well start with the Harvard of chef schools. We walked around the campus, and Chris liked the looks of the place. How could you not? It was beautiful. There were some issues, though. To get into CIA the competition was fierce, and they had very exacting standards. You had to have worked in a restaurant. You had to have earned good grades. You had to fulfill all sorts of criteria—and certainly not be a convicted felon. It should have been hopeless. But "hopeless" isn't a word we use in our family. Was it "hopeless" when my grandfather went up to Yankee Stadium a week after Babe Ruth set the single-season homerun record to try to get him to come to Trenton?

Chris and I went to see the Culinary Institute admissions director, and on our way into her office I noticed a portrait hanging on the wall of the reception area.

"Who is that guy in the painting?" I asked her as soon as I could. (I just wanted to verify.)

"That's Jim Robinson," she said, surprised by the question. "He's an Honorary Trustee of the Culinary Institute."

"Thank you very much," I said, and looked up to God, smiling.

Jim Robinson was my boss. He was the CEO of American Express. I'm not going to say we were pals, but our relationship was good enough that I could go to him about Chris. When it came to getting help for my kids I was and still am shameless. So I went in and told Jim the story, and I can never thank him enough for being so open and receptive. I came out of the closet with regard to Chris. I'd never made a big deal about what we had been through as a family. I had only shared that story with a very small number of people. It was painful. It was awkward. I'm sure in talking to Jim I shed a tear or two. But Jim was very sensitive and helped out and, in the end, Chris got into the school. To this day I'm grateful for his kindness and his help. I'll never forget what he did.

Not only did Chris get into the school, but he also graduated on time. There were no issues with his

performance. He was into it and learned well, showing obvious talent in the kitchen. Just think of it—to
go from doing time as a convicted felon to graduating
from the Culinary Institute of America! I was very emotional attending his graduation ceremony and hearing
what a promising young chef he was. It being a culinary
institute, they of course offered us up a load of great
food, and we were all in high spirits. I'll never forget the
moment of graduation. Just like at West Point, when the
cadets all throw their hats into the air, at the Culinary
Institute of America the new graduates all toss their
chef hats way up in the air. It was something beautiful
to behold.

"Jeez, we made it!" I told myself at the graduation.
"We got through the tough part."

I had a party to celebrate Chris's triumph and his
new job working as maître d' at the Metropolitan
Opera restaurant. We gathered a whole group of friends
at my club in New York, the Columbus Club, but, come
to think of it, those were my friends I invited. As I look
back, the party was probably more for me than it was
for him. Of the 200 people we invited, easily 150 of
them were my friends rather than Chris's friends. I
wanted all my friends to see we had made it. That was
nothing but selfish of me.

It only took a few months before Chris told me he
didn't want to work at the Metropolitan Opera restaurant

anymore and planned to take a restaurant job in New Jersey. I was stunned. It was like all the good feeling was being taken away from me, that all the progress I thought we'd made was an illusion.

What could I say? What could I do? I didn't know how to talk to my son anymore. Chris took one job in New Jersey and then another and another. When he was in prison I had seen him every week, but by this point I slipped out of my pay-attention mode. I was devastated. I figured that I had done everything I could to give the kid a chance, and if he wanted to throw that all away, how was I supposed to stop him?

"I want to be a physical trainer," Chris told me one day.

"But you're a great chef," I protested. "You graduated from the Harvard of chef schools."

It was pointless. He wanted nothing more to do with the restaurant business. Now he wanted to work as a physical trainer. We had come so far, and now he was up to his old ways again. Our relationship became very fragile. We hardly talked. When he started to slip up and repeat his old patterns I let that drive my heart rather than making my heart drive the circumstances. I stopped paying attention.

Chris ended up marrying a woman named Stephanie, but the ceremony brought me no joy. I felt like a stranger—that was how much distance had come between Chris and me. On the day of the wedding I came straight from work and didn't even wear a tux. I was not asked to say anything at the wedding. My son Jay was best man to Chris, and his sister Leslie was also in the wedding, but they had no place for me. I didn't make a toast when it came time for that. I felt like an outcast. It was one of the strangest and most disturbing days of my life.

But Chris asked me for help again after that, and I did my best to set him up. With his background at the Culinary Institute and his knowledge of working out, I tried to hook him up with the biggest diet doctor in New York City, Howard Shapiro, author of the *Picture Perfect Weight Loss* series of books, a very warm and caring individual.

"We can set him up here," Howard said. "I can refer people who need to lose weight to Chris."

It was a perfect opportunity. Chris could have made a fortune and been set for life. All he had to do was follow through. All he had to do was *do* it. But nothing ever came of it. He just wasn't motivated to act. He wouldn't do it. He wanted handouts.

The paradoxes could just drive you nuts. Here was a guy who talked all the time about how to maximize the potential of the human body as he worked overtime to wreck his own body. He was in and out of rehab. His marriage didn't last long. Then he got a job working as a manager at Bally's Total Fitness and seemed to be doing better for a while, making friends and starting a relationship with a woman named Sara.

Then, one day, we were down at the Jersey Shore on vacation when he showed up with the news that he was going to be a father—Sara was pregnant! He pulled out the sonograms, black-and-white pictures of the baby in the uterus—a girl—and we all did our best to be enthusiastic, but it was hard to believe Chris was ready to take on the challenges of fatherhood. He and Sara could barely take care of themselves; in fact, much of the time they couldn't do that. How were they going to take care of a baby girl?

We were right to worry. Being a father didn't change him. They named the girl Elizabeth in honor of Nancy, whose middle name is Elizabeth. We thought that in the end being a father might shock him into realizing that he had to make some changes or else he might not be around to see her grow up. But he never got into being a father. I guess he didn't have much of a role model.

"Chris," I told him. "You and Sara can't take care of your kid. She's two years old. She needs a home. She needs some stability. Your mother and I will take care of her. But you gotta go away, and you gotta stay away this time."

So we took his daughter, Elizabeth. He went away to rehab again then eventually came back and started selling cars in New Jersey, but still we kept Elizabeth. I bought three Envoys from Chris to show support. I dropped in on the car dealership to see how he was doing, and he seemed to be working hard. He even started wearing a tie to work, something he never did.

"Dad, can I have some of your ties?" he asked me, because he knew I had a lot of ties.

I said to myself, *This is good.* They would come get Elizabeth on Sundays for a visit, but Sara was always messed up. She'd smash the car because she was doped up or had some other problem. But Chris kept selling cars for a couple of years. Again we saw his positive, upbeat side. We all wanted to believe that Chris might finally have found some peace and happiness.

Then it all came crashing down again, and he lost the job. I got him another job, this one as a manager of a car dealership, and in less than a week he lost that job too. Again it wasn't his fault—nothing ever was. I finally had truly had enough, and I told him so. I washed my hands of him. I knew it was time for some tough love, and that meant drawing a line.

Time passed, and I found out I was going to be one of the honorees at a dinner before New York's Columbus Day Parade in October 2008. My first thought, even before *My father would be proud of me* or *My grand-father would be so pleased,* was *What about Chris?* It didn't seem right to exclude him nor to include him. What was the point of tough love if you turned out to be a softy? But in the end it just felt wrong not to invite Chris. So I reached out and told him I wanted him and Sara to be there. That was my way of saying I still considered him part of the family. We'd all be gathered as a family for the dinner at one table in the Grand Ballroom of the Waldorf Astoria Hotel in New York.

Jon Corzine, the governor of New Jersey at the time, was sitting at our table that night. I was making the rounds, talking to Governor Corzine and other people, and I kept looking around for Chris. He hadn't showed up. Finally he and Sara arrived late and took their seats, and Chris was so out of it that I thought he might pass out. He kept dropping his head as if holding it up were the greatest physical challenge he had ever faced. I didn't know what to do. I didn't want to make a scene. I didn't want to embarrass my son. But I saw where this was heading: he was messed up and was going to make a spectacle of himself sooner or later, right in front of Governor Corzine.

We all stood up for the National Anthem—or most of us, anyway. Chris was somewhere between a slouch and a sway. My son Jay kept looking at Chris and then back at me, showing me how worried he was. We could all feel the potential for Chris to do something that would embarrass himself and the entire family in front of all these people. You could always tell when Chris was on drugs because he would be sweating like crazy. So I had to do the worst thing I've ever done in my life—it haunts me to this day. The anthem ended, and I got up as casually as I could, walked around the table, and leaned over between Chris and Sara.

"Get up quietly and leave," I whispered into his ear. "I don't think you're in any condition to be here tonight."

He did what I asked. He and Sara got up and left, very obediently, very dutifully. And those were the last words I ever said to him. The last thing I said to my son was "Please leave."

Four weeks later I was at a gala at the Intrepid Sea, Air and Space Museum in Manhattan, and when I checked my messages I saw one from a Linden, New Jersey, police detective. That struck me as weird. I had another message from my son Jay, which I listened to right away.

"Chris is dead," he said. "Chris is dead."

The more I found out about the details, the worse I felt. As it turned out, Chris had been dead since the day before. There were crazy things going on in the little apartment he and Sara had been renting. She found his body and was out of her mind, just walking the streets, not knowing what to do. I'd called my brother, as he'd been doing police work all his life.

"I'm taking care of it," he told me later, "but you don't want to see the body."

Thank God for my brother. Chris had suffered from an enlarged heart and that, in the end, was what had killed him. He looked terrible. My brother arranged for a mortician to pick him up. A few days later we buried him. Nancy and I agreed it wouldn't be appropriate to put a tie on him—he never wore suits. So my wife and I went out and got a red turtleneck sweater and buried Chris in that. We chose red because it was a much more joyful color. It was a small service with just the family. We had an Episcopalian priest come and say some prayers. We took Chris to the cemetery and buried him right. I wanted to make sure he was peaceful at last, because he'd had a life that was anything but peaceful, so we found a spot that was on the side of a hill and bought all the ground around him, making sure nothing could crowd him and he could be at peace.

It all ended as it had played out since he was thirteen years old, but it was the first thirteen years that shaped the next twenty-six. The last time I remember seeing him at peace was when he was laid out, because he'd had such a wretched, unpleasant, unhappy, esteemless life. I don't know whether he thought he could never live up to my expectations or be better than me. God knows; I don't know. I think he never, ever was rehabilitated. I think he faked it enough to get my attention and to get what he wanted. They were all con jobs. He never, ever dealt with the core issue, which was self-esteem. He had a chip on his shoulder, a feeling that something was owed to him because of what was missing in his childhood, and he clung to that feeling no matter what. It played out in variation after variation on a sense of entitlement and a sense that he should never have to work for anything, all because when he was young we never built a foundation that was heartfelt and loving. I could never recover from that.

My son was a drug addict since he was thirteen years old. I thought I did everything I could to help him, but obviously I didn't do enough. I did the things that were structurally correct, but I didn't spend the time or put in the emotion that I should have, and this is where I hope every reader of this book is paying attention. I obviously don't have it to do all over again. But I wish I did. Every time I visit the cemetery where he's buried I cry and say, "I should have spent more time with you, Chris." I gave him money and sent him to rehab and helped him with this and helped him with that, but I needed to do much more, something like the modern-day version of sitting on the dock fishing. That's so important—to put your arm around your kid, to have that time of togetherness. The more kids feel the affection and love that the parent has for them, the more that communication will be possible. But I didn't do that. So I'm a living, breathing cautionary tale.

If Chris had felt there was love, not just a checkbook, who knows? What if I had taken a year off to be with my son? And my other son and daughter? What difference could that have made? I constantly challenge myself about that. I still do to this day. I put so much into my work. I gave so much of myself. People at work waited for me to give them inspiring, motivational speeches, and I did. But I didn't go home and give inspiring, motivational speeches. That sense of failure is something I keep uppermost in my mind all the time. I tell myself: I had to be a real fraud to really be passionate about motivating other people and having a great heart and getting motivated so they became a success, but as soon as I walked in the door of my own home I wasn't that way anymore. There is no question in my mind that if I had been as inspirational and spent as much time at home as I should have, things would have turned out differently. I have no doubt that Chris would be alive today. But I did not do that.

I have to live with that failure—but you don't. There's still time for you. If you take nothing else away from this book, please take this message away: wake up and look at all the important relationships in your life, whether they be with your kids and other family members or with friends or coworkers. These people are part of you. By doing right by your relationships with them, you do right by yourself; you learn about what's important and become more yourself. I got so caught up in my career that I was blind to my kids' needs. A lot of people get too focused on one area of their lives, and that leads to blindness in some other area. People neglect friendships. They neglect colleagues at work and don't offer recognition. The reason you lose children is neglect. The reason you lose friends is neglect. And the reason you lose clients at work is neglect. The way to ward that off is to give your all to caring for other people, being there when they need you, being accessible and open—all the things I didn't do with my son Chris. Pay more attention to your kids. Put down this book right now and go give your kids a hug. If they're asleep, wake 'em. Tell 'em you love 'em. Talk to 'em. Listen to 'em. Stop fooling yourself, and leave no room for regrets later on. Same goes with friends and colleagues. You've got to search inside your heart and figure out what your real relationships are, and you need to find a way to do what's necessary to fix or improve those relationships before it's too late. Do something—do it now! Because you don't want to end up like me, always looking back and wishing you'd done things differently. Do it, and then smile—and enjoy what you've got!

Look Up, Not Down

We all go through tough times that test our ability to rise above negativity and disappointment but ultimately prove to us the power of staying positive and looking for great things to happen for us. For me Chris's death was such a time. My grief knew no bounds, and turning to work was no solution either. This was during the years when I was working for the insurance broker Willis. I made the largest deal in the brokerage industry in a decade the same year Chris died by buying the US insurance brokerage firm Hib, Rogal & Hobbs for more than $2 billion. It might have worked out as a great deal, but I bought HRH at what turned out to be the worst possible time—late 2008.

We announced the deal that June, and the actual transaction went through October 1, 2008, when the financial world was falling apart. Credit markets were closed. The US economy was tanking. "This has been the worst financial crisis since the Great Depression. There is no question about it," New York University economist Mark Gertler, an associate of Federal Reserve Chairman Ben Bernanke, told the *Wall Street Journal* that September 18. And as President George W. Bush put it one week later: "If money isn't loosened up, this sucker could go down."

As this was all going up in smoke, I got the news on November 6 that Chris had died. What had already been a difficult time turned into easily the worst period of my life. But all I knew how to do was keep thinking positive, keep looking for a way forward.

A key part of the HRH deal was to try to clean up some glaring inefficiencies of the company because we discovered that this was a very disjointed company with a lot of disparate units and no integrated culture. HRH had bought more than a hundred different companies and never bothered to integrate them. In Chicago alone there were five separate offices, including Willis. We needed to get those workers all in one place, under one roof, so I had my senior vice president for real estate, Carmine Bilardello, come up with some ideas about where we could find office space at a good price. Carmine and I had worked together for more than thirty years, and countless times he made me look good by turning my crazy ideas into reality. One of the possibilities he mentioned for office space was the Sears Tower, the Chicago landmark that had been the tallest building in the world from 1973 to 1998. I thought we should think big and go for it.

"How much of the Sears Tower is occupied?" I asked Carmine. "I bet there are a lot of vacancies because people are worried about another terrorist attack."

"About 75 percent," he told me.

"Well the guy who owns it must be in trouble, because 25 percent not yielding any cash flow, that has got to be a bitch," I said. "Maybe we've got an opportunity here to get a great rental price. And maybe we can even get the tower named after us."

"Neat idea, but I don't know if they'll do that," he said.

"Carmine, we gotta think big," I said. "The guy's in trouble. The guy needs a triple-A tenant. He needs to go to the bank and say, 'I've got this lease.' C'mon, we've gotta think big here."

In other words, anything is possible if you look up, not down. Always keep that in mind. I was thinking positive and thinking big. So Carmine met with Joe Moinian, part of the group of investors that had bought the building from MetLife in 2004. We were looking to rent 140,000 square feet, which was two and a half floors, about 3.5 percent of the entire building, and Moinian offered us twenty bucks per square foot.

I told Carmine to offer ten bucks. He told me that was way too low. No way we were getting ten, he said. "Just ask," I told him. So we went back and forth, back and forth, and finally Joe Moinian agreed on $14.50 per square foot.

"This is a great deal," Carmine said. "We should do it."

"No," I told him. "We're not gonna do it unless we get the name of the building changed."

So we met again with Joe Moinian.

"I can't change the name of the building unless you give me something for it," he said.

"Well, how much do you want?" I asked him.

"A million dollars a year for the life of the lease."

I looked at him and smiled. "Okay," I said.

He was startled. "It's okay?" he asked.

"Yeah, it's okay," I said. "If you give me a million dollars in business every year, I can give you a million dollars a year for the naming rights."

Soon it was the Willis Tower, not the Sears Tower. We cut the deal. We put the agreement for them to bring in a million a year in business for us into the lease, so, far from having to pay a million for naming rights, we came out way ahead on the deal. If I'd ever been through a time of my life when it would have been easy to buckle under and start making excuses and feeling sorry for myself, that would have been it. But I still had the passion to imagine "Willis" on top of that building and to see an opportunity. My heart told me it was possible to make Willis a great brand in Chicago. I wanted my company's name to be on the tallest building in the Western Hemisphere. If I didn't think it was possible, I wouldn't have asked.

I remember being on the *NBC Evening News* the night of the announcement and being interviewed by Brian Williams. "After all these years, the name is now the Willis Tower," he said. "How do you come along and change the name?"

"I asked," I told him.

Before long United Airlines had stepped in to lease office space in the building, and the occupancy rate in the tower shot up. Then United merged with Continental to become the largest airline in the world, so the largest airline in the world was now located in that tower, and almost all the office space was now occupied. A great deal for everyone involved.

That's a dramatic story to illustrate a simple point: purpose thinking can shift the landscape. In my case it was a challenge to stay positive when my heart was so heavy from the loss of my son, and yet staying positive was what I knew. It was in my blood. It was what got me out of bed every morning and sent me surging through my days. It was reflected in the culture we were able to build at Willis, so that everyone felt it, and that was the key: if it feels like work to stay positive and believe *always* in the potential for amazing things to happen, you're doing something wrong. It should not feel like work; it should feel as natural as breathing. It should feel as inevitable as the sun rising every morning.

That was how it was at another place I worked in the late nineties, an insurance and financial services company called Primerica. My years at Primerica showed me that there is no upper limit on inspiration, no ceiling on how much of yourself you can give to help those around you move into high gear. At Primerica the goal of following your dreams to realize your vision was at the very core of the mission. All around me were people who were looking up, not down and following through to make huge changes in their lives and find themselves able to do things they'd only dreamed of, like traveling to Europe or the Bahamas.

The company was founded in February 1977 as A.L. Williams by a guy named Art Williams, a former high school football coach from Cairo, Georgia, who ended up having a revolutionary impact on the world of life insurance. From 1940 to 1970 the industry was dominated by something called whole life insurance, which didn't just offer a payout in the event of death but amounted to an investment scheme that ate up the individual's often limited resources. Term life insurance, which became more popular after the Tax Equity and Fiscal Responsibility Act of 1981, offered benefits only in the event of your death.

Art's father died prematurely of a heart attack at forty-six with only $5,000 of whole life coverage, leaving his family destitute. Years later a cousin of his told him about term life insurance. Art was in graduate school at Auburn and did a research paper on it. He was stunned to learn that so many people were being persuaded to buy life insurance that wasn't a good choice for them, so he started selling tem life insurance part time while he was coaching football.

Art became a man on a mission. The key to Art's success was that he founded the business based on passion, based on doing the right thing: term insurance helped people with modest incomes make a much more sensible investment. Art and everyone who worked with him felt the extra urgency that comes with knowing you are fighting for a good cause and that you can help people just by educating them about their choices. Once you reached people with the truth of what you were telling them, a light bulb went off, and they tended to get very motivated and, in turn, reached out to others and motivated them.

I'll tell you an individual story that offers a good example of what the company could mean to people. Like so many drawn to Art Williams, my friend John Addison was an ambitious young man eager to work hard to make a better life for himself and his young family. He graduated from the University of Georgia and, for a year and a half, worked in the management training program for an insurance company called Life of Georgia. He enrolled in night school at Georgia State University to earn his MBA and responded to a help-wanted ad for a job that looked risky but at least was closer to his apartment—and his new wife.

"It said, 'Rapidly growing insurance organization looking for bright young college graduates to man home office,'" John remembers now. "I was a college graduate. Bright? I didn't know the answer to that. I went in, and I was offered $19,200 a year to come to the company. I was making $17,000 at Life of Georgia."

John told his employers he was ready to move on to go work for A.L. Williams, and the news caused a stir. The next thing John knew he was called into the office of his boss's boss's boss, a man named Gerald Padgett.

"You are throwing your life away!" Padgett told John. "A.L. Williams is fly-by-night. They're not going to make it. They're under investigation.'"

Padgett sounded a lot of alarms, but he didn't offer John any more money to stay, so John took the plunge and went to work instead for A.L. Williams, which, starting in the mid-eighties, was known as Primerica. (Many years later, when John was co-CEO of Primerica and appearing on Atlanta-area television, Padgett sent him a handwritten note saying, "Thank God you had the good sense not to listen to me." By then Life of Georgia, once a company with two thousand employees, no longer existed.)

Before long Art Williams had almost singlehandedly reshaped the insurance business in the United States. He built his company to the point where he had two hundred thousand agents out selling term life insurance. There was an evangelistic fervor to the movement. These were not people like I'd met in Sandy Weill's Wall Street office when I first landed there. These were middle-class people in towns all over the country, people who were used to scraping by on just enough to live and were now building toward something more. The way it worked was that you could sign up other people to sell as well, and then each time they brought in some money, you'd get a percentage, and if those people signed others up, you got a cut of that as well, all the way out to eleven levels. A former Tennessee school teacher named Ronnie Barnes built up a hierarchy of more than 15,600 reps and, in 1997, was the top earner at $3.1 million.

It only worked to sell if you believed in what you were selling, and these were people who believed passionately. They were selling hope and opportunity. For the first time in their lives they could think about buying a Rolex watch or taking a trip out of the country, something few if any of them had ever done before. It was all about helping other people and helping yourself too. If you wanted to recruit new people, you were as likely to make an impression by showing them your house and having that inspire their dreams as you were by talking about every last detail of how whole life insurance was a scam designed to screw the little guy.

Sandy Weill, my first mentor, bought into A.L. Williams in 1988, and by the mid-nineties he was looking for ways to help the company, now called Primerica, grow and transition. Art Williams was out of the picture by then, having left in July 1990, with the company under something of a cloud because of lax business practices. Primerica needed discipline, but it also needed leadership that understood its traditions. The whole culture of the company was based on inspiration, and Sandy started telling them about someone he had in New York who was their kind of guy, someone who could fire up a crowd and knew all about coming from a humble background.

They all rolled their eyes. Everyone knew Wall Street types were all dull and buttoned down, right? Then they met me. I gave a talk at a conference in Boca Raton, Florida, and had my usual great time firing them up.

"How ya' doin?" I called out in my usual way of introduction. "I'm Joe Plumeri."

Then I made a beeline away from the front of the room right into the thick of the crowd. That always causes a stir. I went for a brisk walk, shaking some hands, saying hello to some people, and worked my way back toward where a couple of people were actually sitting there reading the morning paper, as if I were a CNBC report in the background and not a real person.

"Put the paper down and move up to the front of the room," I challenged them, and they were a little startled to be singled out like that, but they put down their newspapers.

By then I had the attention of the room. I did what I always do—I looked them square in the eye and spoke from my heart. I wanted to grab them and make sure they were with me, so I went to my ace in the hole. I told that room full of people the story of my father having quintuple bypass surgery at age seventy-eight, him lying there in bed pale and unsteady looking, and waving me off when I told him I'd get him a house in Florida so he could go down there and relax.

"'Relax?'" I shouted to the room in Boca Raton, quoting my father. "'I don't want to relax!'"

No, he wanted to bring a minor league baseball team to Trenton, and that was exactly what he did. This was a kind of passion and determination every single person in that room could understand. This was a kind of optimism and crazy belief everyone in the Primerica family had lived for himself or herself and talked up to others. I was speaking their language, the language of look up, not down.

Art Williams had left the company because, as good as he was at motivating, he had a poor record on compliance issues. Once he left, however, the heart of the company was gone. There was no leadership. "We'd had almost a revolving door of CEOs," John Addison told me. "You know how you have the employee of the month? It was, who was the CEO of the month? They had been through this new vision and that new vision, this new vision, that new vision, and people were kind of like, *Yeah, okay, right.*"

Sandy kept throwing person after person down to Atlanta to run, it and they all came back in body bags. This was a unique challenge, requiring all the vision and experience and organizational ability required to run a major company but also the ability to fire people up and keep them fired up with evangelical fervor and passion. One of the cardinal truths about leadership that you always need to keep in mind is that nature abhors a vacuum. In the absence of a common vision, in the absence of leadership, everybody will supply their own vision and their own leadership, and the result will be a divided, scattered company where true teamwork and common vision are out of the question. Bad cultures start in the absence of a common vision.

I think leadership always starts with listening to the people you would lead and doing more than *trying* to understand them, but instead really taking on that challenge so you *get* them—you *get* what they're about, *get* what drives them, *get* their hopes and dreams. That is no easy thing. There are a lot of traps you can fall into even if you're trying your utmost to engage with people and make them feel comfortable. So many good people had gone to work for Primerica, either as part timers or full timers. Many of them had never had a chance to develop their business sense or their awareness of how a crisp, coordinated company could function. It was my job to educate them. But it was also my job to honor and respect the tradition that had built up long before I came aboard, a tradition of giving people hope for better lives in the future. I was there to get them excited about a bright future for Primerica and a bright future for themselves. I was there to motivate them just by being myself, a working-class guy from Trenton who grew up with his father driving him around town on Sundays and telling him, "If you work hard, anything is possible."

I loved connecting with these people. It was exciting to realize that I could reach them and educate them. I could inspire them to go beyond their old ideas of what was possible for themselves and their families. But I also had to look out for signs of pushing people too far, expecting too much out of them. We all have our own weaknesses, and that was always mine: I expected everyone to be as gung ho as I always am. I expected people to be as passionate as I am. I expected people to work as many hours as I do. In some ways I was like the former star player who becomes a coach or manager and has trouble relating to players who don't share his frenzied commitment. But with time I learned to be more alert to signs that I was rubbing people the wrong way with my relentless good cheer and optimism. I learned to laugh it off if people asked me just to give it a rest now and then. One of the warning signs comes when you have a meeting at which you know you weren't at your best, where you lost your audience, but everyone comes up to you afterward to tell you how good it was. That shows you they're just telling you what they think you want to hear. It's the same at home. You know when your kids or your spouse are offering you a heartfelt compliment and when they're just going through the motions.

This was not a job where you sank or swam based on what you did while holed up in your big corner office. No, we were constantly out and about. I hit the road with John Addison and others, and we would talk to groups around the country along with the heads of the various hierarchies to pump everyone up. We would pack the Georgia Dome with thirty to forty thousand people for conventions, and we had a great time, and so did every person there. It was all about getting excited about life. We'd call people up on stage, and they'd come bounding up and hug us and they'd cry. This was their moment. Usually they would run down with their partner, and this was their chance to get some recognition for all they had accomplished. They would run up this ramp to the tune of really joyful, celebratory music to hug us and take a picture. It was just unbelievable. We'd do this for hours. It was all about recognizing these people and how much work and vision they had put into what we were doing. It was all about living the dream. It was all about them hearing their names and being recognized as somebody who was special in life. Everybody needs that sometimes. Afterward they would wait in line, hundreds of them, to get a picture with me. I couldn't believe it.

"Why would you stand in line for hours to take a picture with me?" I asked sometimes.

"Because you give us hope that our future will be better," I was told.

It wasn't about me, Joe. It was about them looking up, not down. It was about them having a picture with the head of the company and being able to show friends and family that the top guy knew them. I felt a deep sense of joy and satisfaction at Primerica knowing that I could make such a profound difference in peoples' lives. When you're around people who are passionate, that comes back to you. When I speak to an energetic audience, that gives me energy. Their appetite was so great to make better lives for themselves that it boomeranged back to me. Again and again they and their honest and passionate belief in making a better life for themselves inspired me.

When people ask me what was the most fun I ever had as a CEO, I tell them Primerica because of the direct effect I had in so many lives. Time and time again, whether at the Georgia Dome or the Philadelphia Convention Center or hundreds of other venues just like them all over the country, I would put on a show, and no one left one of those nights without feeling the passion, the emotion, the heart. One time John Addison came up to me after I'd been on stage for hours and held out a cape for me, just as they would do for James Brown, the Godfather of Soul, at the end of one of his marathon performances on stage. We all had a good laugh about that.

Everyone has ego, and everyone has some greed inside of them; that's how we're wired as humans. The question is: What is more powerful in making you who you are? Is it ego? Is it greed? Or is it a willingness to please? If the willingness to please comes first, if it's a stronger motivator than ego or greed, then you are the kind of worker I want on my team. That's how *I* am. I would go give a speech to six people because I have a deep-seated willingness to please—I love that I can fire people up, inspire them, get them excited. That in turn feeds my ego, which is nice—everyone needs a little of that now and then. But it's not the needs of the ego calling the shots; that's secondary. If you please people and your ego is nourished, then greed can enter the mix; if you do the work, if you come through and produce, you deserve to be rewarded for your efforts. You deserve a payday. If the greed takes over, then you have a major problem. The greed needs to be held in check. It needs to rank third among the three hierarchies of life.

If you get somebody who comes to you and says, "Look what I did! Look what I did, man!" and is truly excited about the work they have done for you, you love that. You love those people. They're so eager to have you say "Great job." That's what recognition is—it's a willingness to please. And then when you hug them, they get an ego boost, so you pleased them, you hugged them, and then they got paid. Or if it was the people at Primerica, they might end up with a plane trip. But it went in that order. Always it started with recognition, like when people would come up to get their awards at one of our gatherings, and they'd be so overjoyed at that recognition they would be crying. Talk about tears of happiness! I was the one getting the press write-ups, but it was only because so many good people in the Primerica family had passion and heart and we could create some excitement together.

"The moment Joseph J. Plumeri II bounds into the spotlight at the Philadelphia Convention Center, the crowd erupts in a raucous ovation," *Business Week* wrote in its 1998 article calling me the "apostle" of life insurance. "No doubt many of the 4,500 people on hand have caught his act before. Nattily attired in grey pinstripes with matching tie and pocket square, he plants himself center stage and opens his arms in a hey-look-me-over gesture. 'He's a stud,' someone shouts as Plumeri, a short, stocky fifty-three-year-old, saunters stage right in super-slow motion. 'It's a cool walk,' he says, getting a big laugh. 'I learned it in the old neighborhood.'"

Art Williams had been smart about using technology to communicate with his people. The company was growing like crazy in the mid-1980s, which was great, but it also made it exponentially harder to keep in touch with all the new people and to make sure everyone was on the same page. So A.L. Williams ended up being one of two companies in Atlanta to have its own private satellite network so they could beam the signal to people anywhere in the country and have Williams or others talk directly to the leaders and rank and file of the company. By the time I joined the company the switch had been made to DirecTV, so everyone had those little DirecTV satellite dishes and could tune in to our show. This was long before the days of high-speed Internet, when this kind of interactivity is now taken for granted, and back then it seemed amazing to people.

"The thing most executives fear most in life is a microphone," John Addison likes to say. "For Joe one of his happiest moments is if there's a live microphone."

I can't deny it. My show was once a month for two hours and would be beamed out via satellite to more than two hundred thousand people. John did the show three weeks out of the month, and the fourth Monday of the month it was my turn, and I just hoped I could maintain the high energy John brought to the show. At first I thought it was silly. I didn't believe anyone would watch. But they did. I developed a following. Busloads of people would come from far away to Atlanta to be on the television show, and I'd interview them.

I had all kinds of fun with the show. One month I might talk about the top ten things that excited me, and they would all be upbeat aspects of what was going on with the company. The next month I might have another top person in the company on with me. If I did something unusual on my show, I'd hear about it from dozens and dozens of people. I was always looking for new ways to inspire people, so one time I had my father on the show to tell the story about how he revived Trenton by getting a baseball stadium built and bringing the Trenton Thunder to town. My father loved everything about Primerica, and in fact, he wanted to get involved himself. He became an agent and started his own hierarchy. He was such a natural that he worked his way up to regional vice president, and at one of our annual conventions I personally bestowed the RVP title on him. It was really cool. The crowd loved it! That's the best kind of inspiration there is—when you inspire your own father.

Just to show you how passionate people were, how seriously they took their connection to what I was telling them, even though my father's death came well after I left the company, they held a special memorial ceremony for him. Hundreds of Primerica people gathered at Waterfront Park in Trenton, John Addison among them, and gave my mother and me a bronzed statue of my father with the inscription, "The dream lives on." What wonderful people!

The challenge from my first days at Primerica was to impose some discipline and accountability. It was hard, I won't lie. A lot of key people fought me on it. But in the end we were able to instigate a lot of changes that prepared the company to move forward later, after I was gone. As it happened, the regulatory world started changing dramatically, but Primerica had no problem because of the discipline we'd imposed. We implemented an Office of Supervisory Jurisdiction to help oversee the sales force. We implemented a new way of selling, needs-based selling, with a Financial Needs Analysis that presented a whole series of questions like, "Do you have kids?," "Do you want to send them to college?," and "When do you want to retire?" People tell you what they need, and you can give them informed advice to meet the needs they've outlined for you. That's needs-based selling, versus old-time, Willy Loman selling, which is "I've got a suitcase full of brushes, and I'm going to tell you why you need that brush. I'm going to sell you this whether you need it or not."

The definition of value was always very difficult to explain. How do you sum that up? Steve Barger, who worked with me at Smith Barney as well as Primerica, came up with the idea of the "value gap." It was very simple: the difference between what a person can do for themselves and what you can do for them. Think about it: if they can do it for themselves, then what do they need you for? You provide no value. The wider the gap, the more important you are in the relationship, the more value you represent—and the more you could charge. Defining it as the "value gap" was a good way to stay focused on providing that value, which led us to needs-based selling. We were one of the early pioneers of needs-based selling, and later, when the regulatory agencies cracked down, there was nothing they could say to us because we were only selling what the clients needed. That's the right way to do business, and it makes selling pure. We made all these changes that were very uncomfortable at the time, but thank God we did them when we didn't have to do them. At first people didn't like it. But it was the right thing to do, and it became a part of the culture. And then when the financial world blew up, the company was positioned.

Working together with the Primerica team energized and inspired me. Because it was middle America, it reminded me of my own roots and where I came from, so I was able to mirror my own experience of growing out of the neighborhoods of North Trenton and help other people do the same, which was why it was a great fit for me. But as emotionally satisfying as the job was and as pleased as I was to have boosted earnings so dramatically, you couldn't give speech after speech to thousands of people without sooner or later being ready for a change. I was fifty-seven years old, and I knew that if I was going to try something else, that was the time. Five years was enough, so I left in 1999, feeling great knowing I was leaving the company in such good hands under the leadership of co-CEOs John Addison and Rick Williams.

A decade later Primerica went public—and CNBC called it the most successful IPO of 2010. Primerica, once you've lived it, is always a part of you. It's part of who I am to this day. I loved the hope and belief that hung in the air at those rallies we had. I loved the can-do spirit and the insistence on always believing that you can pull off the difficult or the impossible, if you look up, not down. Why *not* believe? Why *not* go for it? Why *not* stay positive and let good things happen to you—or great things? The people I met in the Primerica family will always be close to my heart. Even long after I'd left the company I was still constantly reminded of what we had set in motion. I remember my third year in the job, 1997, when we had our annual convention at the Georgia Dome in Atlanta and I told more than forty thousand people, "If this isn't your passion, what you're doing now, then go find your passion. Don't do something every day with no passion and no purpose."

Years later I'd chartered a helicopter in New York and was out there on the helipad, getting ready to board, when the helicopter pilot came running out so he could hug me.

"I love you, man," he told me, and he said it like he meant it.

"Great, thanks," I said.

It was one of those one-seater choppers, where you've got to get strapped in, and as I was sitting there I was just stunned. The guy was named Chris Pasucci, but I kept turning it over in my head and trying to place him or figure out why he was such a fan. Finally I leaned forward to ask him. "How do you know me?" I shouted over the noise of the rotor.

"I went to the Primerica convention in 1997," he shouted back. "You said if that wasn't my passion, then

go find my passion. I knew my passion was flying heli-
copters and getting my own business one day. So I went
for it. And guess what? This is my helicopter, I'm running my own business, I'm happy, and it's all because
of you."

Talk about your great examples of look up, not
down! When people say I'm a motivational speaker, I
tell them, no, I'm not. Moti-
vational speaking is fast food.
It might get people revved up
for a few minutes, maybe an
hour or two, but it doesn't last.
What does last is inspiration.

If you can reach inside of
someone and really connect
so that the message resonates
with them and becomes their own, then you can rewire
them so that they will have energy and passion to work
toward a goal.

> If you can reach inside of someone and really connect so that the message resonates with them and becomes their own, then you can rewire them so that they will have energy and passion to work toward a goal.

That helicopter pilot was just one of many who
emerged from those Primerica rallies deeply inspired to
make a better life. Inspiration comes from within. It's
self-sustaining. My Primerica years left a strong impression on me because they reinforced what I already
knew, which was that the only way to reach people is
to connect with them through your heart, to be honest

and direct and real with them. A good speech is nice. But the applause dies down quickly. Adulation goes away. People forget. Everyone knows the word *vision*, but they don't *see it*. They know the word *passion*, but they don't *feel it*. They know the word *courage*, but they don't *fight for it*. They all know the words, but they don't know the music. Saying the words doesn't mean you feel them. The music lies in the heart, which drives all these emotions, which is where the words come from. If they hear the music, that comes from the heart, and that keeps on playing. If you inspire, that's forever.

Principle 6

Play in Traffic

All the themes I've pursued in this book funnel down to this essential truth: if you don't get off your butt and get out in the world and mix with people, you're always going to miss out. If you don't show yourself, make new friends, revive old relationships, expose yourself to new ideas or new ways of thinking, or just be there to take advantage of the sweet gift of serendipity, then reading this book and getting fired up about finding your passion and living by your heart won't help you at all. Not one bit. For that you need to get out there and *live*. You need to go out there and take chances and risks. That might mean you wind up with a scrape or two, but you can learn from those scrapes and emerge stronger. For that you need to play in traffic, as I like to call it, not be on the Internet, but actually see, touch, and talk to people. I've told stories throughout this book that have made the point in countless different ways: playing in traffic has worked for me, and it will work for you too.

It's another way of saying, "Always show up"—knock on the door, get yourself seen, and when you're in the door, show up emotionally, 100 percent, put everything you have into being there and taking advantage of the moment. If somebody asks you to go to a meeting, go! You're never wasting the time. Go take the meeting! For people who go through the motions, who are looking to check a box, they can skip this advice. It's all about going through life with your heart leading the way and taking a meeting with a feeling of certainty, a total confidence deep down inside that something wonderful is about to happen.

I say you're never wasting your time because the risk of sitting through a dull meeting is far less than the gain that comes when a meeting pays off for you in a big way. You never know for sure ahead of time which meeting is going to be a bad meeting and which one will be surprisingly dynamic and important until you actually play in traffic and go to that meeting. So of course you're going to run into meetings that are not all that productive for you—that's okay. No one should expect to bat 1,000. You're not going to hit a home run every time. Babe Ruth hit sixty home runs in 1927, but he struck out eighty-nine times that year too. I've been to many meetings where someone said I had to go see somebody, so I did, and it turned out to be an absolute disaster, but I couldn't know that ahead of time. I had to try. One time someone suggested I fly all the way to the other side of the world to take a meeting in Yichang, China. That's about as far out of my way as I could go. But I made the trip and wound up with an account working on the Three Gorges Dam across the Yangtze River, the largest power station in the world and a mind-bogglingly large-scale project that involved relocating more than a million people away from the Yangtze River Valley to other parts of the country. I took the meeting. I landed the account. That's playing in traffic.

Even when I was a young kid starting out in law school, I was playing in traffic. That was what I was doing as an eager, clueless kid knocking on doors to try to land a job in a law firm, and I ended up inside the Carter, Berlind & Weill offices at 55 Broad Street. I'm not saying this is always easy. It takes really being courageous and really having an unshakable belief in the power of your own potential, but when I knocked on the door and landed that first meeting with Sandy Weill, I gave it my best shot. Sandy liked my moxie, but the point was that there I was in front of him: he had to do something with me. So even though I felt totally deflated when I found out I'd made a big mistake in thinking this was a law firm, even though I felt foolish and my ears burned, there I was.

It's all about maintaining an awareness deep down of how little you really know. Confidence is a good thing, but arrogance will always do you in sooner or later, and taking the meeting is a philosophy that goes together with never thinking you have it all figured out. I could never have predicted that he'd be curious enough about my potential to give me a shot. He saw that I believed in myself and wanted to see whether I knew something the outside world didn't. He liked that I'd had the grit to hang in there even after I'd embarrassed myself, so knocking on that one door led to all these other doors opening up for me for decades to come. Sure, I made a whopper of a mistake. I get laughs to this day when I tell that story. It could easily have happened that Sandy shooed me out of his office with a smirk and added to my embarrassment with a cutting remark about how I needed to get a clue. Instead, he gave me a job. I learned and worked hard, and a whole world of opportunity opened up to me. But you know what? Even if Sandy had laughed in my face, so what? Even if I'd slunk out of that office feeling like a nitwit, so what? I'd have kept knocking on doors. I'd have kept trying to make something happen. I'd have kept playing in traffic.

Because a "no" is just a no and never matters later on. Think about it: the opposite of "no" is "on"—like, "It's on!" You can strike out six times out of ten and be a great major league hitter, and you can strike out ninety-nine times out of a hundred in business, and if the one time in a hundred amounts to a big enough score, then hey, you're a winner. Anything good that has ever happened to me in life occurred because I got out of the house and engaged in life. Playing in traffic is a nice way to say, *Go engage in life*—go put yourself in the mix, out and about, among people, taking in events, bouncing off anything and everything. Put yourself in the middle of all that stuff, so if anything is going to happen, you're there when it does.

The biggest single risk of life in the Internet age is to convince yourself that letting your fingers dance over a keyboard or thumbing your smartphone amounts to engaging in life. It does not. Trolling on Facebook and hitting LIKE on five different vacation pictures posted by your second cousin or former college roommate might make you feel for an instant or two like you are connecting with people. You are not. Now, don't get me wrong: I'm not antitechnology—far from it. I say go for it and have fun if you enjoy that kind of thing. Have your moments of enjoyment. But that's not going to get you anywhere that matters. If you're interested in getting to the next chapter in your life, finding your next passion and doing something special, that's not going to cut it. For that you need to get out in the world.

Look, we all have moments when we're depressed or demoralized. We all feel sometimes like everything is stacked against us, everything is going wrong, and it's pointless to do anything but give up because we're doomed to failure and disappointment. It can even feel like the universe—or God—is taking a personal interest in making our lives miserable. We all get kicked in the chest—or further south in the anatomy—with a feeling of certainty that we're down on our luck and there's no point in fighting that.

Those are the best of all moments to go play in traffic. It might or might not make you feel better. It might or might not lead to new opportunities or reshuffle the deck of your life to make it all feel different. But what's certain is that if you don't get your butt out the door, you know you've got no shot at recasting your lot. That's true even if the unemployment rate is rising quickly and the whole country is in a panic as it was during the so-called Great Recession of 2008–2009, when the US housing market collapsed so suddenly that we sent the entire world into recession. So what? Get out and go see people!

My father never talked to me about playing in traffic. There was no need. I saw firsthand the way the man lived his life. I observed a guy who didn't sit around the house sleeping or watching TV or listening to LPs on the turntable but a guy who was always out, scaring up a deal, searching to make something happen, angling to be relevant. I observed a guy who was always showing up. He'd invite me to come along with him when I was a kid, and sometimes, if I had no sports practice or was a little bored, I'd spend the day with him. It would just be function after function after function. He was something between a politician and a pseudo-politician, and it was what he did.

They'd have a picnic for the Polish American Society, and we'd go to that and eat kielbasa and listen to an oom-pah band playing polka tunes. We'd go straight from that to another picnic, this one for the Italian American Sportsman's Club, and we'd be playing bocce ball and waiting for the spaghetti-eating contest. It was endless. My dad would always be showing up, and everybody would know him. He was out there, playing in traffic. If you grew up with that, if you saw a man who was always out there trying to make something happen, always heading from one event to the next, that stayed with you. Those impressions, coupled with your own sense of ambition, added up to: Play in traffic!

I actually think the whole American experience has been all about playing in traffic. My grandfather and countless other immigrants came here to play in traffic.

They scraped together passage on a ship to come see what they could accomplish in the New World. They could live the American Dream and do things they couldn't do in Italy or France or Germany or Sweden. Even though they wanted to keep their traditions and what they learned from them, they came here to build on those traditions and to create the American experience. So the whole American experience is about playing in traffic and inventing things and being creative and getting out there and doing it. In the land of opportunity everybody was free to go out and play in traffic.

Playing in traffic isn't just about reaching for the stars and hoping for great things to happen. Sometimes playing in traffic is all about getting out there and getting involved, putting your butt on the line, helping to salvage a bad situation or at least to clean up a mess and make it less of a problem or less of a disaster. In my time at Willis I was given the bad news that a major client, Ted Leonsis, owner of the Washington Wizards and Washington Capitals, was unhappy and we might be losing him.

"It'd be helpful if you called him," the broker told me.

"Okay," I said.

So I called Ted. But this is a chapter about playing in traffic, not playing with the telephone. "You're an important client, Ted, and I'm concerned about what I've been hearing," I told Leonsis on the phone.

"Thanks, Joe," he said.

"Would it be helpful if I came down to Washington and we met and talked it over in person?" I asked.

"It would be very helpful," he said. "You would do that?"

"Absolutely," I said.

There are more arduous tasks than popping down to DC on the train, I am happy to admit. It takes less than three hours on the Acela Express, so in nothing flat I was knocking on the front door of Leonsis's office on F Street Northwest in Washington, eight blocks from the White House. Before I could even give my name to the receptionist, a guy who looked familiar came over to me, smiling.

"Hi Joe," he said.

"Do I know you?" I asked him.

"Yeah, I worked for you at Shearson Lehman Brothers," he said.

"Well, this is unbelievable!" I said.

We talked a little about old times, working together at Shearson Lehman, people we both knew. We were both smiling and chuckling over some of those memories.

"Joe, I told Ted all about you," he said. "I told him what a great guy you are."

"Well, thank you." I told him.

Riding down on the Acela, I was just sure I was walking into a hostile meeting. But this wasn't a hostile meeting at all. Ted greeted me with a smile and shook my hand warmly.

"I've been hearing good things about you," he said.

We sat down and talked sports and talked business and talked life and finally got around to talking insurance. We chatted about all sorts of things. I got back on the train and was home in New York in three hours and had a smile on my face the whole time. Ted called me a few days later. "I want you to know you're going to keep the account," he told me. "You're keeping the account because I know you. You came here personally, and any CEO that would come here personally and show me the account is that important, that counts big for me. That made me feel good."

I can't tell you how many times somebody has called me and said, "Joe, we've got this account that we're not sure about, and I'm sure they'd be real impressed if you called them." Whenever possible I'd go see the person and press the flesh because going the extra mile always makes that much more of a difference. Playing in traffic can be about trying to make a save, or it can be turning around what looks like a negative and turning it into a positive. Other times playing in traffic can mean going for it in a big way, throwing the "Hail Mary" pass because you've got the gumption, the spirit, the balls to go for a big score. I played in traffic when I went into a meeting with the Sears Tower people with the idea of renaming it Willis Tower. That was putting Willis in the mix. That was pushing the action.

A lot of times I talk to people who are looking for a job or a new business opportunity to pursue, and they'll tell me, usually with an awkward laugh, "Joe, I'm waiting for my ship to come in." That's an old-time expression that I've always enjoyed. It's evocative. It's colorful. It's also passive.

"How many ships did you *send out?*" I ask anyone who says that to me.

They always look confused.

"You said you're waiting for your ship to come in," I say. "If some ships are going to come in, don't you have to send some out first?"

All of a sudden it dawns on them: well, hell, if there are no ships out there, none are going to come in. By playing in traffic you're putting your own ship out there. The more you see, the more opportunities you're going to have for something to happen, and that holds true if you're twenty or forty or sixty.

I'm doing it right now. I'm playing in traffic. I'm practicing what I preach. And something will come out of all of this. I come home at night and am excited to talk about my day with my wife, Susan, who for the last seven years has given me the support and love and direction I've needed at a very difficult time in my life. She asks what I was doing, and I say, "Playing in traffic!" I have five, six, seven, eight meetings a day, where people have this or that idea for me to consider. Maybe they have a hedge fund and they say, "Joe, let me tell you what I'm doing, maybe there is something we could do together." Or they're in private equity and want to know what I think of this or that and maybe I'd like to get involved. Somebody called me up and said, "Joe, I'm interested in buying a baseball team—I need some advice." So I saw the guy and talked his ear off about owning a baseball team. Or if a kid wants advice, I see the kid. Whatever the case may be, I see everybody. I always say, *Go take the meeting.* It's about showing up, and it's about showing up emotionally as well. If somebody asks you to a meeting, go! You're never wasting your time. It's about having a feeling in your heart that if you go, something is going to happen. You might go to 100 meetings and nothing happens, and then at the 101st meeting something will happen and you're glad you went to all 101 of those meetings. That's playing in traffic!

I return calls. I never say, "I don't know that guy. I'm not going to return his call." I call everybody back.

I do that because I know from experience that the more people you talk to, the more you engage in life, the more things you show up for, the more new possibilities are going to be generated. That keeps you excited and passionate, having new opportunities emerge all the time. It keeps you interested and engaged. And you never know when something truly amazing is going to happen that might be a one in a million but would never show up for you if you weren't out playing in traffic.

Let's say you're the owner of a small business. I met a guy named Jim who had a small fleet of trucks and diversified so he also had storage facilities and even a little data processing. Then the economy took a sudden nosedive, and the housing market went haywire. No one was selling their houses, and no one was moving. Jim's business was in trouble. He worked his tail off for years trying to save it. He spent sleepless nights racking his mind for ideas on what else to try in order to keep it afloat, and he tried countless different strategies, but in the end it was just not humanly possible to save that business. Jim had to let it go and start looking for a Plan B. He decided to get into real estate when the market was down and he could work hard and establish himself, putting himself in a great position for when the market picked up and then he would have a foothold. But real estate is a competitive racket. A lot of people are out there ready to sell houses. So what do you do? You go to every meeting or social event you can think of to go to. You work seven days a week, every week. You go door to door handing out flyers. Jim did all that and more. He made things happen. He got his butt out the door. And, last I heard, he was doing just fine—if you want to buy a house in northern California, let me know and I'll hook you up with Jim. You'll love the guy. He's a fighter. He's a winner.

Woody Allen once said that "eighty percent of success is showing up." I'd call that estimate low. I'd put it north of 90 percent, easy. People need to appreciate and understand that if you want to do something special, if you want to get ahead, you've got to have a vision; you've got to have a dream and the passion that comes with it. But none of that is going to happen unless you get out and *do* something.

One of the pioneers of the US feminist movement was Gloria Steinem, cofounder of *Ms.* magazine. When she was getting her start in the early 1960s she went undercover as a Playboy bunny at the New York Playboy Club and wrote about it for *Show* magazine. Talk about getting off your butt and going out and taking action! She had every reason to worry that she would be considered unserious because she had been a Playboy bunny. She had no idea what would come of the assignment. But she went for it, and the result was an article that caused a sensation and put her on the map. She went into detail about sexual demands made of the girls and made other revelations that forever changed how people thought of Playboy bunnies. Still, she paid a price. She had written for *Esquire* and other national magazines before the article, but even so, other feminists dismissed her, all because she had been a "bunny." But she kept playing in traffic, kept making things happen, and within a decade had founded *Ms.*, which became one of the most influential magazines for the women's movement.

Who are your heroes? Who are the men and women who have inspired you in the past? Or inspire you now? Chances are, if you look into it and give it some thought, they were people who went out and played in traffic. Oprah did a lot of playing in traffic on her way to establishing herself as probably the most important media mogul in the world. The examples go on and on and on and on—and it's worth thinking about those examples, worth learning from them and taking something away so that you too will get out the door and play in traffic. In a day and age when there are more people graduating from college than there are jobs, you can't wait for something to happen. You can't be passive. You can't be reactive. You need to knock on doors and get out there and make something happen. You need to play in traffic.

Five years ago a guy who was honored by the Columbus Foundation asked me to introduce him at the big awards dinner. I said, sure, glad to do it. The night of the dinner the president of the foundation came over to me and said, "Joe, that was a great speech—we forgot all about you, sorry to say. But would you be an honoree next year?" That wasn't why I was there, angling for an honor. But hey, I wasn't going to turn him down. I said, sure. So a year later there I was at the same dinner, giving another speech. The president of the foundation liked that one too. So two years later I was the grand marshal. If I had stayed home and not gone out there to give the speech introducing my friend, none of that would have happened. If I'd said, *I'm going to sit on my couch and watch the ball game tonight*, none of that would have happened. But life's too short!

One time I read a survey of eighty-year-old CEOs and former CEOs. (Luckily I wasn't one of them.) The survey asked these veterans, "What would you do differently?" I found it very thought provoking. The number-one answer the octogenarians gave was they wished they had taken more risks. The second-most popular answer was they wished they'd had more fun. And the number-three answer was they regretted not spending more time working to build monuments to what they believed. In short, they were all saying they had not played in traffic enough, because playing in traffic is about taking risks, knowingly and gladly; it's all about having fun, because it's always more fun to get out there and be engaged and involved than it is to sit on the sidelines. And playing in traffic is also about building monuments to the things in life that really matter.

The only way to make progress on leaving something behind is to go for it and go for it all the way, to shake the great pinball machine of life and try to get it going. That's how you work to pass things on to the next generation, like the beautiful Jackie Robinson Museum in New York, opening in 2015, that I have been lucky enough to play a role in helping make possible by doing some fund-raising at the request of Rachel Robinson, Jackie's widow. After I read that survey of CEOs I vowed that I wouldn't be talking about any of those regrets, so that's why I'm focusing more now on what I want to leave behind, what I want people to remember about what I did with my life, and what my beliefs and my passion were. All of that funnels down to the constant of everything depending on playing in traffic.

I mentioned in Chapter 2 that when I was CEO of Willis I instituted the ultimate open-door policy. Except for conference rooms and closets, we would have no closed doors at Willis. Everyone, including me, worked in an office with no door. That was a symbol of our commitment to communication, accountability, and transparency, but it was also something else—an invitation for everyone who worked there to play in traffic. You can still play in traffic when you have a job and a career. You can still pull away from the computer screen to go mix with people, get to know strangers, take part in discussions that change your perspective. Playing in traffic is a way of life; it's a mindset that keeps you fresh and shakes up your way of thinking and feeling. Playing in traffic is taking the extra step, going the extra mile, putting a little of yourself in your actions in a way people don't do nearly often enough.

One thing I did at Willis was to take part of every day to write handwritten notes to different people in the company, singling them out for something special they'd done or just letting them know their hard work was not lost on me, the guy with the title. This was something I'd always done, just like Mom had taught me, and I decided I was just going to be me. So I used to send "Joe notes," which I saw as a way of helping to fight the company's tendency to be very impersonal. When I first got there no one would communicate with each other. This was a global company with seventeen thousand people working for it worldwide, and I must have sent thirty, forty, fifty notes a weekend. They caused a commotion. They blew people away. People would have them framed up on the wall. They couldn't believe I took the time to send a handwritten note. That made them feel good, made them feel special. But you know what? A note is something special. You frame it and save it because it has meaning and permanence. I've never seen an e-mail framed. I've never seen a text framed. And I don't think I ever will. I get e-mails all the time now, like, "Nice to see you today!" I'm not going to frame that. That does not reach me or anyone else on a deep level.

It's really important for people to understand that the essence of life is engagement. You've got to get out and *engage*. I don't care how technical or technological you are, ultimately you've got to engage people face to face. Part of that process can be picking up the phone or—I cringe to write this—sending a text or e-mail, but this is only a first step to getting out there in the real world. The text or e-mail setting up the call doesn't mean a damn thing if you don't get out there and follow up.

One difference in how newspapers get read nowadays is that a lot of people only read them online, which means you see a headline and click on a link and read that article—or read half of it and get bored—but that's that. It was different in the days when people sat with a newspaper in their hands. You might spot an article on the front page, read the first few paragraphs, and then had to flip to a page deep inside the paper to read the jump, and as you did that, often you spotted other headlines that grabbed your attention and maybe you stopped and read that article too. That's what it's like to play in traffic and get out there: you might run into someone one table over at the restaurant where you're having lunch, or, like me in Paris when my wife and I ran into Henry Kravis, you might happen to cross paths with a guy who has your next job in his back pocket.

It's a thread running throughout life that nothing ever really happens without somebody playing in traffic. That can be anything you can do that gets you out and about and puts your name out there so people say, "Hey, who was that guy?" or "What was the name of that woman who just dropped by?" You want them to notice you and remember you and think of you later when a tantalizing opportunity presents itself. You want to get that call from the person with a great offer to make, and if it's not right for you or you're not available, there's never any harm in turning someone down. It's always good to be in demand. It's never a bad thing to be wanted.

Whenever I get a chance when I'm back in New York I love to grab lunch or dinner at Ristorante San Pietro on 54th Street near Madison. Why do I love the place so much? Well, obviously the food's great or else I wouldn't go there. As *New York Magazine* wrote, "The food here—much of it using ingredients grown on chef Antonio Bruno's family farm back in Salerno—could bring tears to a mafioso's eyes." But San Pietro offers much more than delicious meals. Every time I walk in, owner Gerardo Bruno stops by my table, and we talk like the old friends we are. He sets a great tone and gives the place a great atmosphere. There are always a lot of people you know there, and it's a great way to mix, a great way to see and be seen, a great way to play in traffic. Really, it's just a variation on what made everyone love the great TV show *Cheers*. Ted Danson as bartender Sam Malone served customers like Norm and Cliff and Frasier who wanted to come in and check out the action and wanted to have a place "where everybody knows your name and they're always glad you came."

In a lot of parts of the country you don't even have neighborhood watering holes like the *Cheers* bar anymore where you can stop off and get a bite to eat, watch a few innings of the ball game, and shoot the breeze with the regulars and anyone else in earshot, if the mood strikes. All this mania for fast food, drive-thru fast food, stuffing your face on the go even if that means filling up on junk—we've lost something, losing out on neighborhood joints in favor of McDonald's and KFC and Burger King.

So you need to look for alternatives. If you're in a smaller town or regional city and looking to play in traffic, you can join the local Chamber of Commerce, not just to get on their mailing list and add one more set of e-mails to your in box but to also take part in meetings, speak up and be noticed, make friends and make contacts. That's playing in traffic. Service club organizations like the Rotary Club and the Lions Club and the Kiwanis Club, all founded around a century ago, have grown into large international organizations, topped by Rotary with 1.2 million members worldwide. The Jaycees, as the US Junior Chamber is popularly known, offers another service club possibility. I tend to think of the Rotary and the others as being outdated, more 1950s than twenty-first century, but there are a lot of young people all over the world joining and giving the organization fresh energy and direction. Not long ago I was on a flight to Europe and was surprised to see a whole group of young people all on their way to Portugal for an international meeting of Rotary Club members. Look up your local club and go check it out. That might be the thing for you, the perfect way to go play in traffic.

Religious gathering places are another good option for getting out there and mixing. Religious organizations offer many options for volunteering, or you can join other volunteer organizations, which will mean you can do good as you're also playing in traffic. Put whatever skills you might have to work to give something back. If you played a little baseball and know the game, maybe volunteer to coach Little League. Or if soccer or basketball is your sport, then coach one of those. When it comes to playing in traffic, getting involved with youth sports is a great option. Kids have parents and parents have jobs and parents own companies. A sideline conversation with someone who casually brings up a business opportunity as you watch the game together will always count for a million times more than getting an e-mail or a Tweet.

Everything good that has happened to me has occurred on a relationship basis because of time spent together face to face. Nothing that happens via the Internet will ever replace that kind of relationship. The Internet may help you find opportunities for relationships. You get on the Internet and find somebody that's interested in selling something or has an interesting thing going and wants others to get involved, but it all culminates with a phone call or a conversation that takes place in person. From what I've heard, the same goes for e-dating: you might plug in all kinds of information to eHarmony or match.com, and, hey, maybe their logarithms or whatever will line you up with the perfect future mate for you, and you can then exchange all kinds of e-mails, even talk on the phone, but until you get out there and meet face to face, you'll never know. Not until you've looked into each other's eyes and listened to each other, making allowances for awkward timing or other adjustments, will you really have any clue whether this is a promising potential relationship. Think about it: every time you meet a couple and get around to asking them how they met, they always have a story. This coincidence led to that coincidence. This disastrous evening led to them seeing each other in a different light. Each of these stories has its own quirky details, but each and every one of them is all about going out and doing something, about people getting off their butts and giving something a try, mixing it up with no idea of whether anything will come of it. Each of these stories, in other words, is all about playing in traffic.

Do the unexpected. Surprise others, and surprise yourself. Do some things and take some risks, whether they be personal risks or things you need to do in order to see your dreams realized. You need to have a sense of childlike enthusiasm about everything you do. The problem with adults is that the childlike enthusiasm goes away because you become easily embarrassed or intimidated. Children don't have that kind of fear. I don't think you can put yourself into what you call a serendipitous situation unless you have that childlike sense of flair and enthusiasm that doesn't fear being embarrassed. Playing in traffic keeps it fresh. It keeps it fun and exciting and interesting. It keeps you on your toes, open and alert, engaged and inspired.

Playing it safe does have its advantages: it's one way to limit variables. But you might as well just lie down in your coffin right now if you want to live that way. I say, just go for it. If you play in traffic, you might make a fool of yourself, the way I did when I knocked on Sandy Weill's door all those years ago. But you know what? It wasn't so bad looking like a fool. My ears burned a little. I wanted to slink down in my chair. But I got a job out of it. I got a career out of it. And I've never looked back. Playing in traffic—showing up for the meeting, making the call, putting yourself on the line, giving it a shot—that causes serendipity. That puts you in a position where great things can happen. Play in traffic. Make a difference. I'm here to say you can make it work for you and live a joyous, rich, fulfilled life. Treat every day of your life like it's your *whole* life because, you know what? It is. Go have fun, and let that take you where it will. Go play in traffic!

Paste this list on your refrigerator door or the bulletin board in your office, right across from family pictures.

PLAY IN TRAFFIC, LIKE JOE

- fitness clubs
- sports leagues
- recreational activities like bowling or bocce ball
- social or business clubs like Kiwanis International
- business organizations like the Junior Chamber of Commerce
- religious organizations
- public lectures
- concerts
- political groups to meet likeminded people
- restaurants or lunch spots
- alumni trips or other organized group travel

Principle 7

Make Your Heart Your Teleprompter

You can use Google to find the show times of a movie you want to see or learn about an author you want to read. You can seek out restaurant reviews. You can Google a million facts about a million things. You can spend your entire life at the computer or on your smartphone, Googling everything. But you *cannot* Google where to find your heart. You *cannot* Google where to find your passion. All of that you need to find on your own. All of that you locate not through technology but through your heart, which can guide you through every moment of your life far better than any other compass you will ever find. Technology should be used on behalf of people, not instead of people.

Let's bring old-school values to the new school. Let's bring yesterday's feelings to today's technology. Let's start with the emotion and passion to shape our vision of who we are and who we want to be. Let's demand more of ourselves and more of our leaders and take advantage of every opportunity that comes up to communicate to each other—and to ourselves—the difference between just talking about living with passion, purpose, and heart, just paying lip service, and actively living the truth of putting your heart first. This is not always easy—demanding more. As Winston Churchill said, "Courage is what it takes to stand up and speak; courage is also what it takes to sit down and listen." The path of least resistance is to go with the flow and get swept along by the currents swirling around you and not think for yourself or feel for yourself. Insisting on change takes character, grit, and courage.

When Mitt Romney was running for president in 2012 he came to see me in my New York office. He'd heard I tended to do well with a crowd and had a fun, people-pleasing style of public speaking that generated a lot of emotion.

"You're a great speaker," he told me. "Is there anything you can tell me?"

I smiled.

"Remember that no one who listens to you give a

speech will remember later *what* you said," I told him. "They'll remember how you made them feel."

I had his attention.

"That's the way I speak," I told Mitt. "I have people all the time who will say to me, 'Joe, that speech you gave was great,' and if I ask them what I said, they don't remember. They just remember they laughed and smiled and walked out of the auditorium or the Georgia Dome feeling inspired and excited."

We've become a Teleprompter society. A great speaker today is defined as someone who reads well. To me that's not a great speaker. A great speaker is somebody who can speak from their heart and transfer that passion to somebody else and make them feel good. Harry Truman standing on the back of the train had no Teleprompter—he spoke in honest, plainspoken language, and he spoke directly to the people, directly from his heart. A Teleprompter can tell me what I'm supposed to say, but it does that with absolutely no personality, character, or emotion. I prefer to think of it this way: my Teleprompter is my heart! If your Teleprompter is your heart, it will gush forever. You will never, ever run out of passion or words.

One reason why it's always going to work better to have your heart be your Teleprompter is that you'll remind yourself of what you really think and feel. You'll put your true self out there, and you'll get a reaction from real people, one that is human and heartfelt, and you'll know they have an authentic sense of who you are, even if sometimes the reactions you inspire can be wary or antagonistic at first. That's okay. People will come around in the end when you follow your heart and peer into the truth of the direction it offers you.

My friend Joe Califano followed his heart when he served as Secretary of Health, Education and Welfare after being appointed by Jimmy Carter in 1977. Joe reorganized the department and started important initiatives in areas like childhood immunization and alcoholism. But his most startling action was to take on cigarette smoking, which in the 1970s was about as established a part of American life as baseball and apple pie. Joe knew it would be unpopular to take on smoking, but he also knew it was the right thing to do—cigarettes could kill you. So in January 1978 he launched a major crackdown, calling cigarette smoking "slow-motion suicide" and proposing then-unheard-of ideas like banning smoking in government buildings and commercial aircraft. That month the Associated Press reported,

> Califano, a heavy smoker himself until kicking the habit in 1975, announced details of the anti-smoking program on the fourteenth anniversary of the now

famous Surgeon General's report on smoking and health.

On Tuesday, the Tobacco Institute held a news conference to attack the government's new campaign without waiting to find out what it involved. The head of the lobbying group said there was nothing Califano could tell the public that it doesn't already know. He said the institute also maintains that no one has proved smoking is hazardous to health.

William F. Dwyer, an institute Vice President, charged Califano has "a prohibitionist mentality" and was using his public power "in pursuit of a private hobby."

A private hobby. That's how much Joe was seen as coming out of left field. But he knew the truth and didn't care about the criticism. Joe smoked for twenty-eight years until he finally quit after his son asked him to stop. Joe kicked the habit as a birthday gift to his son. Then he became a man with a purpose and was brave and bold in taking actions that in effect began the modern antismoking movement as we know it. Gradually it picked up steam and led to a complete revolution in attitudes toward smoking. For his troubles Joe got himself fired by Jimmy Carter, but it was worth it, doing what he knew was the right thing.

Look at the impact he has had. Would you ever have believed that there would be no smoking in Irish pubs? Or restaurants in Paris? Or in New York City? Or on airplanes? Isn't it funny how no one has smoked on a flight in this country for many years, and yet they still have those little NO SMOKING lights, as if no one can quite believe smoking is now prohibited? Joe Califano took the long view and put the needs of all before his own need to keep his job and avoid getting fired.

That kind of bravery and willingness to buck trends has become more and more unusual. Many people seem to accept that with all the technological tools at our disposal we're rushing into a future in which we are more and more like computers ourselves—heads stuffed full of information, analytical capacity maxed out all the time, emotion stifled and ignored. Sounds like a nightmare to me. We all know that the best futuristic movies always end up asking the question, sooner or later, of whether the robots can become human. Isaac Asimov worked that ground with his 1950 book *I, Robot*, featuring a "robopsychologist" named Susan Calvin, and Will Smith starred in a film adaption of the movie with lines like, "You're not suggesting that this robot be treated as human, are you?"

Why the fascination with robots acting human? Because we all understand that being human, having heart, which is what makes us human, counts for far more than having information at your fingertips or being able to make lightning-quick calculations or to remember everything under the sun except what you feel. We all grasp that it is our hearts that matter above all, but collectively we are lacking answers to the question of what to do about this obvious problem confronting us, this drift toward the heartless and automatic and away from passion and vision and purpose.

I remember during the 1987 stock market crash I went on the squawk box with all my brokers, not because I had any great news to deliver and not because I could hide the fact that it was a terrible day, but just so I could be there for them. I wanted to speak to our people along with the other executives to reassure them and to allay their fears. There was emotion in the air, and it was all negative emotion, like fear and worry, and I could feel it. I let my heart be my Teleprompter to tell me what to say, and the words gushed forth.

Unless you have leadership or an atmosphere that is hopeful, fear will always take the day because people can always find a focus for their fears. They are afraid of losing their jobs. They are afraid of losing their houses. They are afraid of their neighbors or the guy one lane over on the highway flashing them a dirty look. They are afraid of what might happen in the rest of the world. They are afraid of what they can't control. People want to get past their fear, but they're finding that harder and harder to do. They're finding it harder and harder to focus on positive examples and instead look to distract themselves in a thousand ways. But hope trumps fear every time.

Look at the things that make people happy today. Who are the most popular people in our society? The entertainers, celebrities, actors, and movie stars— because they all offer a form of escape. They all make people forget about everyday life. Celebrity status today is usually accorded not to politicians, not to academicians, not to scientists, but to Jay Z and LeBron. In the last presidential election Mitt Romney got around 60 million votes and Obama around 65 million, yet on some nights *American Idol* contestants receive more than 100 million votes. What does that tell you?

The pace of change is so fast, the need to update so relentless that we're losing our bearings. We're trying to navigate without the fixed points that have guided us for generations. I'm here to say that maybe now and then we should pause to take a deep breath. Maybe every once in a while we can take a break from doing everything faster and quicker so as to reflect on who we are and where we are going.

Maybe every once in a while we can take a break from doing everything faster and quicker so as to reflect on who we are and where we are going.

If we choose to live in a society where information is so easy to get but also so easy to discard, so easy to acquire but also so hard to understand, then are we doomed to forever lower our sights? I offer a powerful alternative: let's start with emotion and passion and allow that to shape our vision of who we are and who we want to be. It's worked for me, and I hope it will work for you too.

Listen, I'm not saying it's always easy when you open your heart. People choose to distract themselves from their real feelings because it can be painful and difficult to let the real emotion come out. It can be confusing and unpredictable. I know, for me, all these years since we lost Chris, no matter how good I might be feeling on a given day, like on my wedding day in Florida when Susan and I were married, still I felt undercurrents of other painful emotions. One of the worst days of my life was my son Chris's wedding, because he was in such bad shape then that he and I could hardly have a real relationship and I'd given up on him; I'd distanced myself. I wasn't asked to give a toast at my own son's wedding.

I vowed that I would learn from the mistakes I made with Chris and do my best to be there for my son and daughter. I vowed to let my heart be my Teleprompter, to let it guide me, and my heart did not fail me. Jay and I have a great relationship, at this point like buddies as much as father and son. I cried tears of joy when Jay asked me to stand next to him on his wedding day. He had plenty of buddies he could have asked, but he chose me. He was telling me with that gesture that he considered me not only his father but also a good friend, and he wanted to find a new way to communicate that. He was telling me he loved me and knew how much I loved him. You couldn't ask for a better present from your son, a better acknowledgment, and the best part of all was that during the ceremony I held Jay's six-month-old baby son, Jackson, in my arms, so we had three generations of Plumeri men together at the altar. That was one of the greatest moments of my life. For Jay to feel it was important that I be his best man meant that all of the heart that was missing from my relationship with Chris was there in my relationship with Jay. Thanks for that, Jay! And seven years later I was able to return the favor: Jay was my best man at my April 2014 wedding to Susan Edgerton.

Learning from your mistakes means never talking yourself into believing you've learned more than you really have. That's where following your heart, letting it guide you, plays so important a role: your heart doesn't sit still for rationalizations or excuses. I'm far from perfect. I know I don't have all the answers. I know I don't get to pat myself on the back. No, I need to keep the pain of loss in mind always and use it as a lever to focus myself on doing the right thing.

There's no room for complacency when you've lost a son. But you also can't stop trying to enjoy the kids you have left. That would be wrong. I was so proud of Jay when he worked so hard to open a restaurant called Plumeri at 121 Hudson Street in the Tribeca neighborhood of Lower Manhattan. The joy of being in business with my son was just terrific. We'd go in on a Saturday to taste every single item on the menu, from pizza to lasagna and linguini, until everything was just right. I even had my mother come check out the dishes, because no one knows Italian cooking like my ma.

We got a nice little review in the *New York Times*, but our timing stunk. The restaurant was at the corner of North Moore and Hudson, just six blocks uptown from Chambers Street, practically in the shadow of the World Trade Center towers. We were aiming to open in September 2001 and pushed back our launch, but even so, it was as bad a time as you could possibly have to open a new restaurant down there. Everything in lower Manhattan was shut down. The streets were empty. People loved the look of the place and loved the food, but there just weren't enough customers. It never got off the ground the way we wanted it to. It went out of business because of 9/11, and we'd spent a lot of money.

But the money didn't matter; it was nothing compared to the relationship that it fostered between Jay and me.

Jay learned from that experience and moved on and is doing great. He lives in East Hampton and he and his wife, Rowaida, operate a restaurant there called Race Lane that is doing very well—and has delicious food.

My daughter Leslie has always wanted to help other people, and for years she was a counselor at Outward Bound. She went through very rigorous training and could have chosen easy programs like those for business executives or tourists. Instead, she chose to work with adjudicated kids—you know, the kids who go before the court and get a choice between doing time or going with her to do Outward Bound. They considered their options, took one look at her—she's got blonde hair, blue eyes, and a dynamite smile—and they all said they wanted to go with her. So the next thing they knew they were out in the wilderness for two weeks with her, wishing they had gone to jail instead. The transformation of these kids was amazing, all just based on the limited experiences most of them had up until that time. In the beginning they all tried to be badasses. They all had attitude. They were kings of the street, but they soon found out that in the wilderness they weren't so bad. I'd ask Leslie, "Should I be worried?" and she'd only laugh and tell me, "Are you kidding? I'm their ticket out of there. Nothing's going to happen to me!" After two weeks, when they finished this grueling but exciting program of challenges, their attitudes went away. I was really proud of Leslie when she did that. She could have taken the easy route, but instead, she followed her heart. I smile and get teary eyed every time I think of her bravery and generosity in helping so many kids.

If you let your heart be your Teleprompter, it can lead to good decisions in business as well. Early on in my time at Willis I decided we ought to offer benefits to the life partners of anyone working for us, and we implemented partner benefits at a time when that was very unusual. We weren't responding to pressure. We weren't looking for PR. We just wanted to do what was right. I trusted my heart, and my heart told me that if someone works for the company and gives his or her all, they deserve the same benefits for their loved ones as anyone else at the company, regardless of sexual orientation.

I was just doing what felt right to me. I was just doing what felt fair. I was just trusting my gut and my heart. I didn't commission any human resources people to give me reams of research on what other companies were doing in this area. I didn't put my finger to the wind. I just acted. Because it felt right to me. You never know the impact you are going to have on people or how you might shape their lives. Sometimes you find out later. Sometimes you never find out. Every day you do your thing and try to be a good role model, and you never know whether something comes of it.

Years later I was in for a surprise. I was invited to a big wedding at the Four Seasons Hotel, a lavish affair with more than seven hundred people. The famous lawyer David Boies performed the ceremony. Bryan Eure, who worked with us at Willis, was marrying a guy named Bill White, both good friends of mine. The law had recently been changed in New York to allow same-sex marriages, and everyone was in high spirits. Then it came time for speeches.

"I want to thank one special person," Bryan told the seven hundred people gathered for the joyous occasion. "Without that person I wouldn't be here. The reason I'm at Willis and the reason I came to New York was the only insurance broker who gave partnership benefits to gay and lesbian couples—Joe Plumeri. He had the courage to do that. I wouldn't be in New York and I wouldn't be at Willis and I wouldn't be standing here tonight if not for Joe."

I was floored. I never knew that. I was so moved, it made me cry.

It can be almost comical watching the herd instinct in the corporate world. When Willis made the step we made on this issue, we were almost alone; now everyone is doing it, and whether they're doing what they think is right or just looking for positive newspaper coverage, either way I guess it's progress. In fact, in a March 2013 article the *New York Times* wrote,

> When the Human Rights Campaign approached Lloyd Blankfein, Goldman Sachs's chairman and chief executive, a few years ago about making a short commercial in support of same-sex marriage, Mr. Blankfein said he had the impression he'd be one of a number of prominent business executives taking a public stand.
>
> As it turned out, he was the only one. "It was a little lonely out there," he said. It's not lonely anymore. This week, Goldman Sachs was one of more than 100 corporations that lodged their support for same-sex marriage in two briefs filed with the Supreme Court. "I think people wanted to attach themselves to what may be the last great civil rights issue of our time," Mr. Blankfein said.

I read that article and said to myself: *Isn't this interesting?* Blankfein and Goldman Sachs have been so maligned, so it was good to see him getting a little positive publicity. His whole point of view is that this is not a personal matter; it's just good business because there happen to be lot of gays in the workforce, a lot of gays at Goldman Sachs in management positions, so from a business point of view corporations should sponsor this. All of a sudden hundreds and hundreds of corporations wanted to join the cause of supporting marriage equality because it was good for business. I could have told them that a dozen years ago. Or their hearts could have told them if they had only been listening to their own hearts instead of forever chasing after the latest expert advice or rational analysis. Trust your heart and you can have great experiences like being at a beautiful wedding and suddenly being singled out as the reason those two people are together. That made me feel great. I loved crying those tears of joy.

Listening to your heart can make you impulsive. I love being impulsive. One time I was asked to head up to the College of Saint Rose in Albany, New York, to inspire the students there. It's a small private college. The nuns there reminded me of my grammar school days and the nuns there who had taught me life lessons by heart. I felt like hugging each and every one of them—and I did. A friend of mine is chairman of the board of the school and explained to me that the students tend to be from working-class families, the kind of families who have never sent anyone to college before, so the students reflect the hopes and dreams of an entire family. That to me is the core of what this country should be about: dreaming about making a better life. So I went up there to speak to their annual business luncheon, and that went over so well that they asked me to come back and give a commencement address.

As with my home town of Trenton, Albany is a northeastern city in transition. Albany is not what it used to be. Though it is the state capital of New York, it has seen a lot of urban decline. A generation ago you could visit the parks of the city and there would be bands playing on Sunday afternoons and people in nice clothes milling around on green grass and trimmed trees. When I went there to give my speech at St. Rose's I saw that some neighborhoods were broken down and some parks were run down and, from what I heard, infested with drug dealers.

I loved giving that graduation speech in May 2006 because these are my people, just like back in the neighborhood in Trenton. You could see that the graduates were the sons and daughters of bricklayers, bus drivers, artisans—honest working people with big hearts. I was wound up good that day, and they must have interrupted me with applause a good four or five dozen times. They knew I was one of them, and they were in a mood to be inspired, which any reader of this book knows by now is my thing.

A beloved figure on campus had died a week before my speech. Bob Bellizzi, longtime manager of the College of St. Rose's baseball team and also a former manager of the Albany Senators, had been battling leukemia for a decade and finally lost his battle. I'd been hearing about him and liking what I heard. He was my kind of guy. He kept it positive, even during his fight with leukemia, and talked a lot about passion and teamwork and seeing baseball as a way to learn about life. He was so beloved that the entire college community was saddened by his death. Coincidentally, his daughter was graduating that day. His dying hope was to find a way to build a baseball stadium for St. Rose, which was badly in need of one.

So during my commencement speech I improvised. My heart was my Teleprompter, and it told me to connect with my audience and to connect with the memory of this beloved figure. I talked to them about my father and his dream of building a ballpark for Trenton. I told them the stories I've told you, right through to the happy ending of how my father succeeded against long, long odds and how the result revitalized Trenton. It wasn't about baseball; it was about passion, and the result was that a downtrodden city was renewed. If not for that boost, Trenton would really have been in trouble, like Albany was. I talked about how proud I was that anyone coming to that ballpark now sees a statue of my dad— and can feel inspired by his example. Then I told them that their Coach Bellizzi sounded a lot of my father.

"I build monuments to [my father] because I believe in him, much like you believe in Coach Bellizzi," I told the crowd, and then continued, "I am so moved by what you have done for me, because you have done it for my father, I would like to help you build a monument to my father and Coach Bellizzi and donate $100,000 in their memory."

The reaction was phenomenal. People were already laughing and crying and cheering during my speech, but now they were amazed and thrilled and thankful all at once. There was this buzz in this crowd, like everyone knew this was a day they would be talking about for years. One by one they started coming up after the speech and asking to talk to me and to give me a hug to say thanks. Dozens more came. After picking up their diplomas that day, half the graduating students stopped by to thank me. I stood up and hugged every single one of them. It was unbelievable, a day I'll never forget.

The way it all worked out, my pledge to donate $100,000 ended up turning into a million when all was said and done, but it was well worth it. Working with Albany mayor Jerry Jennings, chairman of the board of trustees Dan Nolan, and school president Mark Sullivan, the plan to build a ball field quickly grew into a much more sweeping vision of a public-private partnership to construct an entire sports complex where a drug-infested city park had been. We decided it was better to aim high and establish facilities that both the college and the community could use to help keep kids active and playing sports instead of providing a place where drug dealers and homeless people could congregate.

So then what happened? This was all in motion when I got the horrible news that my son Chris had died. The Albany project turned into a way to honor his memory. The Christian Plumeri Sports Complex gives young people a place to be healthy and play ball. The whole college uses it. The whole community uses it. The day it opened and we dedicated this beautiful gleaming, new facility I was not the only one who cried tears of joy. We all did together. There is a bust there of my son and what his life was about and why I didn't want his life to be in vain but instead so people could see what this field was about and other kids could learn from that. It doesn't bring Chris back. Nothing does. But it does bring hope to a lot of lives.

That project, like so much that matters in life, took years to develop. There was nothing simple about it. One thing about electronic Teleprompters is that they are fast and easy. They eliminate variables.

If you're speaking from and following your heart, sometimes you might be overcome by emotion, and other times you might be momentarily at a loss. Listening to your heart is not an instant fix. Sometimes it takes time.

We need to practice every single day of our lives, really tuning into the truth of our hearts. The more we listen to our hearts, the better our heart's message comes through loud and clear and the more likely we are to be able to follow what our heart is telling us. It's easy to fall out of practice. It's easy to develop bad habits, like clicking from e-mail to e-mail in a hurry, never quite feeling anything except the numbing sensation of being rushed for time. You know what? You're worth taking more time. You're worth letting enough calm and quiet open up so that the background noise fades and you can tune into your heart, loud and clear and in Technicolor. When you do that, your heart will be your Teleprompter. It will show you the way—and believe me, you'll never look back.

> If you're speaking from and following your heart, sometimes you might be overcome by emotion, and other times you might be momentarily at a loss. Listening to your heart is not an instant fix. Sometimes it takes time.

Principle 8

You Gotta
Have a Purpose!

I t's been more than two years now that I've been working on this book project, and when I say working, I
mean putting my heart and soul into it. If you've read
this far, you know me well enough to understand that I
always do that. That's who I am. So in those first weeks
I put my heart and soul into talking through the mate-
rial that I'd develop into this book. It was intense, and
I was on a roll. I thought that at the rate I was going I'd
be done with my book in a few months. But in those
early months the book was a passion. It was a preoc-
cupation. But it had not yet taken on a true sense of
purpose.

It was on a visit to San Diego, looking out at the
waters of the Pacific Ocean spreading out beyond

Coronado Island, that something clicked for me. I'd stood up in front of groups of people for years and told the story of losing my son Chris. I wanted to pass on what I had tried to learn from that wrenching, soul-killing experience and what I hoped others would learn as well. But over that long weekend in San Diego I realized that I needed to open up even more. I needed to put more of myself into telling the story. I needed to find it within myself to be so honest and direct with people, as few if any CEOs had ever been in telling this kind of story, that I could ask them to follow me on the emotional journey as I told this story and to learn from it. That was when this pursuit truly took on a sense of purpose for me.

You've read this far, holding a book or device in your hand, and if you're like people in groups I speak to around the country, chances are you've been doing a lot of nodding your head at the points I've made throughout this book. Early on I told some stories that helped me learn all over again just how much people the world over have the same plumbing. It's just human nature sometimes to get caught up in our differences, to think the little stuff matters more than it does, but in the end, deep down, we're all the same, and we want the same things out of life. I know I made some of you smile when I talked about Grandma's house and all the delicious cakes and candies that would be waiting for us there. I know you could relate to that with examples from your own life about the importance of spelling out for people all that's at stake and all that can be reached if you have the ideas and the passion and the vision. I gave examples from my own life about how I've always believed that you need to cut your own path, even if sometimes it's more difficult that way, even if sometimes it leaves you alone and exposed, because it's the right way to live, and you are going to find yourself rewarded for your initiative.

I don't take it as a big compliment when people respond to these points, because none of it's about me. It's about these ideas. It's about transformation. Most of us already know in our heads the truth of what I'm saying. They know it in their hearts too, even when it's tough to know. The emotion of my chapter on letting sadness teach you was raw at times, blunt and honest, but that was the only way I know how to remember my son Chris, hoping as I do that through my example others will be inspired to take the time to be there for their kids, to be there for the people in their lives, and never to take communication for granted but instead always try to be more present and more open when talking to those you love. If I were standing in front of you talking to you directly, I wouldn't even have to use words to remind you of the lesson to look up, not down because I'd do just that, staring high up in the air, and you'd all get just what I mean.

I could talk all day—and sometimes have—about the essential importance of playing in traffic, getting your butt up out of that chair in front of the computer and being out and about, mixing it up, not always having a plan, sometimes trying something just to try it, sometimes landing face down with a big flopping sound, but it doesn't matter because a "no" or the slap of disappointment never has to stop you or slow you down long, so long as you keep getting out the door and putting yourself in a position for great things to happen. And finally, in the previous chapter I reminded you that when you're powered by your heart, you'll have all the inspiration and direction you'll ever need—if you let your heart be your Teleprompter and you strip away the expected or the scripted in favor of what's inside you, right then and there. The truth and force and beauty of that honest emotion will light a path in front of you and carry you along.

I love it when people react well to these principles because I'm happy for *them*: they're on the verge of stepping up to transform their lives. There are two kinds of people in the world—incrementalists and transformationalists. The first thing you have to do is identify for yourself which you are. It's not always clear. It takes some time to search within. That's something you have to know. I'm a person who believes in transformation. That's what works for me—and I think it will work for you. To transform, you need to leave fears behind, to attack that fear to remove it as a barrier, and to move forward toward the truth of being yourself. Our fears will always limit us—unless we attack them.

The problem is that it's one thing to know in your head that something is right, but it's another to activate an emotional sense of connection to the power of the idea in the here and now. Telling yourself intellectually that you need to do something is a little like deciding to walk halfway to the door, again and again—you can do that a hundred trillion times, and you'll never get to the door. You'll never get anywhere. The question you have to ask yourself is: How do I really be myself? It's a question that can have a million answers if you're raising it as an intellectual exercise, but if instead of kicking around mere *ideas* about yourself you rely on the emotional truth of what feels important to you, then you start making progress.

There are two kinds of people in the world—incrementalists and transformationalists. The first thing you have to do is identify for yourself which you are.

The transformative ingredient is *purpose*. You have to allow yourself to *connect* with a sense of purpose.

Have you ever wondered why people so often use the word "passion" but avoid talking about "emotion"? That's because emotion is nice, but it's not enough; it doesn't make anything happen, doesn't change anything. You see a lot of people who are emotional—they're crazy, they scream, they yell—but that's not passion because there is no purpose in there. The boss who carries on just to carry on or your relative who is annoying and disruptive at the dinner table, just to be disruptive—that's not passion. There is no purpose to that. When you couple emotion together with purpose, *then* you have passion, and that's what makes the world go around. That's why things move. That's how things happen. Things don't move because you're emotional; they move because you combine your emotion with purpose to give you the passion to *make* things move.

Throughout my career—in three decades or so with the companies that became Citigroup, a dozen years as chairman and CEO of Willis, and my most recent chapter at First Data—I have always tried to stir things up. But it has always been with a purpose. At Willis we had large "telepresence" rooms installed in New York, London, Nashville, and other cities around the globe. These rooms weren't like your average video conference. A whole wall in each of the rooms was a high-definition screen. If I were in London, for example, my team in

New York could see me in life-size, head-to-toe display, sort of like when Princess Leia appeared as a hologram to implore Obi-Wan Kenobi to get off his butt in the struggle against the Empire. The only difference was that I wasn't wearing a white dress; I was in a three-piece Italian suit. But I was still imploring my team to fight against long odds to beat our competition.

Sometimes these teleconference meetings about sales, products, and pipelines went on for hours, and I know that some of my people must have emerged from the room battered and bruised, thinking "Plumeri's mad!" I had a pretty good sense that they weren't thinking I was "mad" in the *angry* way but rather the *crazy* way. To them I would always respond, "There's a method to my madness."

It was true. My method was emotion, coupled with purpose, equaling passion. By being so obsessed with the size of our pipelines and the constant need to stay in touch with our existing clients to retain their business and reaching out to new potential clients to win their business, I was leading with purpose. In a sales business it's all about three things: keeping what you have, growing what you have, and getting more of it. My team needed to see how crazed I was about all three. What they saw as madness I saw as purpose. And the proof was in the pudding. A company that was moribund in 2000, when I arrived, with a share price of $3, had a share price of about $42 when I left as chairman in the middle of 2013, an appreciation of 1,400 percent! It happened because we became crazed—emotional, passionate, and purposeful—about keeping what we had, growing what we had, and going out and defeating the Empire to get more. A method to my madness, to be sure!

The exact same thing is true in everyday life. People need to ask themselves when they wake up and start their days: What's my purpose? What's the point of getting up in the morning? What is the point of what I do? It's not about you. It's not about making money. It's not about building a company. It needs to be about more than that to have meaning and to inspire a sense of purpose. For that it has to be about transferring what you feel on to another group of people. They can be called clients. They can be called your kids. They can be called friends. They can be called whatever you want to call them.

I began this chapter sharing with you how much I've focused on writing this book in the two years since I left Willis. There's another reason the momentum slowed: I went back to work! For a guy who has worked constantly, seven days a week, for the past half-century, it's a hard habit to break, even when I know it has wrought major consequences as well. But when I see a true purpose in how I spend my waking hours, it's impossible for me to ignore that North Star.

I've been working since October 2013 as a senior adviser to my old friend Frank Bisignano, a colleague from my Shearson days, who is now chairman and CEO of First Data. It's been a real eye opener for me. First Data, which has about $10 billion in annual revenue and is a member of the Fortune 500, is the largest payment processor in the world. About half of all of the world's credit and debit card transactions are processed through the company, to the tune of about two thousand swipes per second, every hour of every day. That's a lot of the world's flow of money passing along the company's rails.

At first look it's a company all about technology. First Data processes payments and helps people accept payments. If it's a debit card, the bank pays the merchant. It either helps banks issue cards or helps merchants accept them. A company like First Data is fundamental to the daily functioning of the global economy, but for most it's a company you've never heard of. This was a lot to grasp when I first started working with the great team at First Data. Since its origins in 1971, providing processing services to the Mid-America Bancard Association, it has changed, evolved and grown into an international powerhouse. But still, superficially, it appears to the outside like a mass of servers and rails. And yet, First Data is so much more than that.

I let the superficiality fall away and focused on the

real picture: First Data uses technology to do business, but the heart of the company, and the key to its future, was all about its relationships all over the world. First Data has twenty-four thousand employees around the globe, with six million merchant clients who accept credit cards and about five thousand bank clients who maintain accounts for merchants or consumers. Each of its clients is a company—either small or medium and large businesses, or banks—populated by still more millions of people. And at the distant end of the transaction are hundreds of millions of more people—you, me, and our friends and relatives—who use our credit or debit cards on a daily basis. At its heart First Data, which everyone thinks is a technology business, is in fact a people business!

Thinking about First Data in human terms was a revelation. The purpose of First Data, it was apparent, had to be looking at ways to help all those clients out there grow their businesses and, in the case of merchants, improve their quality of life. Think about it: if small businesses employ 30 million people, and 60 to 80 percent of all new jobs come from small businesses, this is the future of the country we're talking about. If small businesses don't grow, enabled by constantly improving technology and the people behind it, the country doesn't grow.

So the purpose of First Data, we all reasoned, is

genuine concern for our clients. If we can supply our merchants with apps and solutions to get better at what they do—everything from tracking time for employees, to inventory, to accounting for their business, to health care, to taxes—then all of that turns what we've all thought of as a simple terminal—that point-of-sale swiping machine on their counters—into a critical tool that can really help their small business grow. Our purpose, then, comes out of genuine concern for small merchants' ability to grow their business. Even in a huge technology company, it turns out that technology is simply the delivery system, and the purpose of that technology enables people to realize their dreams, which helps them grow their businesses. So at the end of the day, with all that technology that First Data has, it still has to be guided by its purpose, and that purpose needs to be something much bigger.

With First Data's purpose defined for all to see, the sky was our limit. If your purpose is genuine concern for your clients, then you're going to win because they're going to be better off. You will do well as a company and do well as a person. The same is true at home. If your purpose is genuine concern for your kids or your friends, then you're going to win too because they're also going to be better off. Purpose coupled together with emotion is what gives you passion. That purpose is to have genuine concern for making a difference in other people's lives.

Earlier in the book I talked about the three qualities that define what kind of worker someone is going to be for you: ego, greed, and a willingness to please. Everyone has those three ingredients. The question is in what order they come. Ego is good. You want someone working with you to have pride and think highly of themselves. Greed is fine too—people work hard, they're talented and capable, and they deserve to be compensated for that work. But the quality you always want to see driving the other two is a willingness to please. Show me that worker who gets excited about his or her work and is thrilled when that work gets a good reception. Any time I'm hiring, if ego or greed are decisive, I look elsewhere. People dominated by ego are all about themselves. People dominated by greed are all about themselves. But a willingness to please will give you the best workers, capable of teamwork and improvement and seeing the larger picture above and beyond their own needs and wants. They get excited about pleasing a client. They get excited about pleasing you. When they do this they are rating themselves on how well they work with others, which is the best of all qualities. As a result, they have genuine concern for others. After all that is achieved, then obviously their ego is satisfied and they get paid. *A willingness to please* is just another way of saying *a sense of purpose*. People like that make the best workers and the best friends; they're the people you want to be around.

The stories I've told in this book have not been focused on me. I was a player in all of them, but they were, for example, really about the people at Primerica who looked to me to help inspire them and make the needed improvements in that company that helped it to go public. The stories were about my father and grandfather, amazing men proud of their Sicilian heritage who loved this country and all the opportunity spread out in front of them. From the first days at Carter, Berlind & Weill to the present day at First Data, the stories were about clients and brokers and people whose lives crossed paths with mine. The only time in all these stories that it was really about me was when I was telling you about my son Chris, and that was a story about my pain, which became my purpose, but much too late. The one time it was about me, tragedy hit me. I had spent more time worrying about my job and my career than I had thinking about my son. My purpose should have been him. My genuine concern should have been him. It wasn't.

Every other story was about others—and about the purpose they found to inspire their work. My purpose to get the Sears Tower renamed the Willis Tower was not about me; it was genuine concern about my company. If we could get the name on that tower, it would be a home run for our brand. When every sales person at First Data adopted genuine concern for their clients, the service they would provide them would be impeccable. I've learned through the years that when I didn't have purpose, I got it wrong. When I did have purpose, anything could happen.

There's a simple story that I thought about the other day that illustrates this point: when you think about the other guy, when you focus your efforts on showing him genuine concern, you win in the end. Early on in my career, when I was working for Carter, Berlind & Weill, the name I'd seen on the sign out front going door to door as a law student, I thought we could try something new that would help our clients do more with their money. This was back in 1971, and at the time, when a client had money in a brokerage account, the money just sat there and earned interest for *us*, not the client. Back in those days we used the clients' money for ourselves and invested it—unheard of, I know, but that's the way it was. It worked, up to a point. But then clients started taking money out of the account and taking it to a bank, where they could negotiate a better return on their investment based on how much money they had. Your return was based on how much negotiating strength you had, meaning the small inves-tor was always at a disadvantage. If you were a little guy, you got whatever rate they gave you.

I started thinking about that little guy and how we could improve his leverage. I had an idea: Why couldn't we at Cogan, Berlind, Weill, and Levitt buy a new certif-icate of deposit every day and bring the big investor and the little investor in at the same rate? The legal depart-ment told me it should be no problem. Although my sec-ondary purpose was to make sure we kept the money at the company, my real purpose was to make sure the little guy got the same rate as the big guy. If they were happy, if they were better off, sooner or later that would be good for us too, but that wasn't even the point—it was a way to show people that they mattered to us.

So I went all over the country raising money. We went everywhere you could think of, and we got a great reaction. People were excited to sign up, and why wouldn't they be? This was good for them. We raised millions of dollars a day from all these people and then every day invested that in one big CD, and no mat-ter how large or small a contribution the investor had made, their return on that investment would be the same. We made our case clearly in the cross-country road show, explaining how we were doing wonderful things for the small guy. We reasoned that it was a great way to invest your money short term until you found something interesting in the market. And by the way, we didn't get paid for CDs. We were raising all that money, and there was no commission on it. Our purpose was to do something good for people, and because of that, they stayed with our company and eventually invested their money—with us.

One of the stops on our road show took us to Miami Beach. The room we spoke to was largely populated by retirees, everyone a silver-haired octogenarian except one guy in the front row with a legal pad who was taking notes. It turned out the guy with the legal pad was from the Securities and Exchange Commission. They slapped a cease-and-desist order on us, and we could no longer do what we were doing. We had to shut it down. But what we were working on was a good idea inspired by our purpose. What we were basically talking about was what we've come to know as a money market fund. I can't tell you I invented the money market fund, but I can tell you that that's exactly what our idea eventually became. A guy named Henry B. R. Brown invented the money market fund in 1972, called the reserve fund, just after I was experimenting with similar ideas, and I had nothing to do with that. But because I had purpose, I was trying to do the same thing Brown did. The point is: If you have purpose and are out there trying to help other people, good things will follow. That road show, and the effort behind it, is a story of purpose and of playing in traffic, and a story showing that anything is possible.

Or I can turn to the world of pro sports for another example. As a diehard Yankee fan, I can't say there were a lot of highlights from the 2014 season, but I was lucky to be there for Derek Jeter's last game at Yankee Stadium. I couldn't get over it. The weather report called for rain, and some people with tickets stayed home. Why would they do that? We're talking about Derek Jeter's last game. What's the worst that can happen? You have to wait out a few drops? C'mon! Jeter's finale was one of the greatest baseball games I've ever seen because it capped off in style one of the all-time amazing careers. Jeter was great—everyone got that—and he was great because it was never about him. People all over the country gave him standing ovations, even in Boston, because it wasn't about him; it was all about the game, it was about winning, and it was about the way he played the game. Why was the guy so respected? He never put on a show. He was never a hot dog. He was being himself because he was enjoying the game, he was enjoying the fans, he was enjoying the environment. Can you imagine? The guy played in thousands of games and never got thrown out of the game? It had to be about the game. So people have to ask: If it's not about you, what *is* it about? What is it that you want to do to make something else better? Or to participate in something else that's better? Derek Jeter knew that, for every year and every game he played.

Like Jeter lacing up his spikes, I always put on one of my best suits when I go out and give a speech. We all have our uniforms that remind us of the team we're playing on. Today First Data is the extraordinary team of professionals around the world that I'm playing on. I'm proud to wear their uniform. When I'm out there, microphone in hand, I give speeches that connect with people because my purpose is to make them feel good. That's my purpose which, therefore, becomes my passion. As always, it's not about me—it's about them, First Data and its clients. If it were about me, they wouldn't respond. I wouldn't get the kind of standing ovations I get even when I'm speaking through my iPad to hundreds of people in a city thousands of miles away.

Recently, while at First Data, I was supposed to go to Chicago to give a speech to five hundred people. My doctor had me on antibiotics and told me I couldn't go. So I called the person running the meeting and said I can't get to Chicago—the doctor told me not to fly. He was very upset because he had an hour and a half slot to fill. I felt bad, so I asked whether maybe he could Skype me into the ballroom. I didn't even know what that meant, but I'd heard the term used before. He talked to his technology people, and they figured out they could use FaceTime to get me hooked up through my iPad to keep the First Data event on schedule. I propped my iPad up on a couple of books, and the crowd in Chicago could just see my face and my hands; in fact, they could see them better than if I had been there live. I gave my presentation with all the passion and emotion that I usually give, but because they could see my face much better, through technology, I was able to connect with the audience and convey my passion even through technology. Then I did the same for a First Data group in Dallas and then a group in Miami, and it worked just as well. That's a way to use technology not *instead* of a person but *on behalf* of a person. Technology is great, but make sure you don't lose yourself, your passion, or your heart.

When I was giving my speech through my iPad the power of being yourself still came across loud and clear. I could only see the part of the audience my iPad showed me, but would you believe, they gave a standing ovation to a screen? The power of being yourself is really the purpose you have and its genuine concern for something else other than you. You can't have the passion to direct yourself to a purpose unless you're genuine. What's the last thing you worry about when you have true purpose in your life? What people think of you. You don't care about that, not for one second, because you no longer are focused only on yourself. You have bigger fish to fry. Your larger purpose means that you care about getting it done, about achieving what you want to achieve, about having the impact you want to have or transforming those emotions you want to transform. With a sense of purpose you can't worry about how you behave, how you're going to look to others, and what they are going to think of you. You don't even ask yourself those questions if your purpose and your genuine concern are real.

Everyone understands this intellectually, but too often something holds them back from making the emotional leap to really *live* this. It's like people who know that smoking is bad for them or that eating bad food will catch up to them sooner or later. Intellectually they know, but they don't make the emotional leap to connect that to their lives and actually make things happen.

Once you make the leap from the intellectual to the emotional, like the great people do, that's when you start to execute and do great things. I saw this happen up close at First Data.

I can't push you over this bridge. I can't force you to make this leap. There really are moments in our lives when the words fade away and it's time simply to act or not act. We've heard the arguments, the rallying cries and the exhortations. At some point we decide to take a step over that bridge and march into a sense of control of our own days and our own hearts. At some point we decide to go from intellectual to emotional, to purpose, to passion, and finally to genuine concern. The bridge that takes us there, that delivers us to the promised land, is called purpose.

How many people agree intellectually that smoking is bad for them but don't emotionally buy into that truth, so they don't stop? Whether you talk about people making New Year's resolutions, or deciding they're going to be a better father, all those things people intellectually agree should happen, why doesn't anything ever actually happen? It's because they don't emotionally make the leap. They never find the sense of purpose.

My whole life has been going from the intellectual to the emotional and letting it all hang out, and that's allowed me to be passionate about everything I've done. I'm a man with a purpose and have been for as long as I can remember. Everybody's got to have a purpose. Corporations have mission statements that purport to reveal what they are all about. In my view a mission statement is mechanical; what's needed is something real: a *purpose* statement that comes from the heart. But to find that purpose, you have to start by committing to having an emotional involvement in whatever you do, whether as a company or as a person. That purpose allows you to make the emotional leap and show genuine concern for whatever you're doing. You'll be yourself and will find a purpose, and that will lead to genuine concern in everything you do. You cannot go through that progression without being yourself. It won't be about who you are and how you behaved and what other people think of you; it will be about that genuine concern. All of it leads to being yourself. If you have a purpose and that purpose is borne out of genuine concern for something or someone other than yourself, then you will in fact be yourself. If it's not about you, then it frees you to be yourself. That's the secret sauce!

Epilogue

This book is not meant to be stashed away on your bookshelf next to your collection of John Grisham or historical novels or your twelve-volume military history of World War II. This book should never be put far away. Keep it close at hand. Consult with it. Make it a day-to-day part of your life, lying right there on your nightstand, easy to revisit whenever you need fresh inspiration or practical advice. You might have a big meeting coming up at work, so you reread Principle 5: Look Up, Not Down. Or during the holidays a relationship with a family member has you concerned, so you reread Principle 4: Let Sadness Teach You. Or you just feel a little down and in need of a lift, so you reread Principle 6: Play in Traffic. Try it—you'll like it! It is my hope that you, the reader, can find ways to incorporate my eight principles into your daily lives. My ideas are merely a guide to help you find your own purpose.

I encourage you to read this book in whatever order and at whatever pace feels right to you. There will be no quizzes! You can skip around all you want. Jump ahead to the last principle first, or content yourself with reading and rereading the first few principles again and again. Also, you're going to want to read sections of the book out loud. Don't fight it. You'll feel the urge, and why not go with it? Call up friends and loved ones or colleagues and read a paragraph or two out loud. Invite people over, serve up coffee and tea or uncork a bottle of red, and take turns reading, and then talk over some of the points. Speak from your hearts. Talk about what's really important to you. Face your fears and come away with new clarity about your passion and your purpose in life. You'll feel more like yourself than you ever have.

Additional materials can also be found at my website, www.joeplumeri.com, where I have made available an interactive worksheet to help you create your game plan and get in touch with your core beliefs, values, and passions. This guide is only the beginning. I want to be inspired by *you*. Share your personal stories, challenges, and successes with me and everyone else at www .joeplumeri.com/shareyourheart. Connect with others online at Facebook and Twitter @JJPlumeri. Go beyond technology and the Internet and get involved in your community as suggested in Principle 6: Play in Traffic. Start your own BYS (Be Yourself) movement in your school, office, meetup group, religious institution, or retirement community. Put down this book and go play in traffic because *anything is possible!*

Applying the Principles

In Principle 1, Everyone Has the Same Plumbing, I ask you to *have the faith and courage to be yourself, to relax and let a little spontaneity and joy into your days.*

CHECKLIST TO BEING YOURSELF
- Be who you are.
- Did you cry today?
- Smile today.
- Laugh today.
- Get passionate today.
- If you did all of those things plus the normal human things, then you were yourself.

Principle 2, Show the Way to Grandma's House, is about creating a clear vision for yourself: *What is your vision of where you are going? What is your passion?*

IF YOUR VISION IS SO STRONG YOU WILL DO WHATEVER IT TAKES TO GET THERE,

- Did you figure out where Grandma's house is for you?
- Are you prepared to do whatever it takes to get there?
- Are roadblocks, difficult times, or friends giving you a hard time?
- When you think it's too hard or too easy then it wasn't real in the first place.
- Paint the picture to endure the trip.

In Principle 3, Cut Your Own Path, the stories of my father and grandfather offer inspiration and belief of their visions. *People who cut their own path are usually fearless. They go beyond limitations. They think for themselves. People who follow the familiar path are less curious. They let someone else clear the way, to overcome their fear for them.*

CHECKLIST FOR CUTTING YOUR OWN PATH
- Were you fearless today?
- Were you limited by your fear?
- If you feel comfortable following someone else's path, then fear has probably gotten in your way and you need to check back in.

In Principle 4, Let Sadness Teach You, I share my personal heartbreak over the loss of my son, Chris, and how I wish I could have made more time for him. *Where you spend your time reflects your purpose. If your week was a pie chart, where do you spend most of your time?* HOW COULD YOU MAKE TIME FOR THE RELATIONSHIPS THAT MATTER TO YOU?

- Pick up the phone and call someone you care about.
- Send a note of appreciation to a friend just because.
- Let people know you genuinely care.
- Get out and do something together in the great outdoors, like sitting on a dock fishing.

In Principle 5, Look Up, Not Down, I share my ideas of leading from the front and not the back. This requires listening with focus, asking questions, and offering wholehearted attention. When you do this you suspend beliefs, judgments, and ideas. In this way you amass accurate information. *Leadership is the relationship you have to someone else. This can be as basic as being a good friend.*

- What leadership roles do you play in:
    - o your family?
    - o your work?

- ○ your community?
- ○ your friendships?
- You have an opportunity and a leadership position to make a difference. If you don't make that difference, then the idea of leading is valueless.
- Do something someone can't do for themselves.

In Principle 6, Play in Traffic, I emphasize the importance of taking the meeting, of getting out there and connecting.

I'VE GIVEN YOU MY LIST OF PLACES WHERE I PLAY IN TRAFFIC, BUT:

- What are yours?
- Where are places in your community where you can connect with others?
- Where would you suggest others play in traffic?

In Principle 7, Make Your Heart Your Teleprompter, I talk about connecting to your heart. You don't need anyone to script you. You don't need to read what you want to say. It just comes out because it's the way you feel. *If you thought about what you were going to say, you scripted yourself. If you didn't feel good because you behaved differently from how you feel, then you didn't follow your heart—you read from a Teleprompter. Don't do that. You'll get acne.*

In Principle 8, You Gotta Have a Purpose, I reminded you that people need to ask themselves: *What is my purpose? What's the point of getting up in the morning? What is the point of what I do?*

Write your own personal mission statement using the following equation:

VISION +BELIEF + PASSION = PURPOSE

- If the vision is the right one, then you'll really believe in it and it will be clear.
- Check out my grandfather and father.
- If you're stumped now, go start from the beginning—find another vision and keep doing it until your purpose is born.

Acknowledgments

S usan, my wife, for loving me and accepting me as I am. And reminding me who I really am every day. You are my biggest fan.

Jay and Leslie, thank you for accepting and loving me for the father I am.

My father, for always encouraging me to "run hard," and my mother for her endless support.

To my brother Butch (Sam), the Sunday rides still continue. Thanks.

Dee Schiavo, for your patience, kindness, and always letting me be myself no matter how tough, rough, and ugly. Your loyalty and kindness have carried me far.

Steve Kettmann, in you I found a writer who got *me*! You understood. You are a person of passion and always willing, no matter what time of day, to go over a thought or phrase that put it all together. Thank you for helping me write my story.

Todd Shuster, my agent, for being in this for the long haul and understanding that for any book to work, it had to be all about me being myself.

Dan Ambrosio, my editor, for having heart and passion and caring about this book as much as I do, and Cisca Schreefel for her diligence and patience working with me down the stretch.

For all those who opposed my unique style of leadership and demand for excellence and passion. Because you smoothed out the edges.

Josh King, who constantly prompted me to write this book. Thank you for support and encouragement through thick and thin. You knew I had something to say.

Carmine Bilardello, who played an incredible role in an incredible story.

To my friend Steve Barger who taught me what value and purpose is.

Henry Kravis, who gave me a chance. What a gamble! You hired me to be myself.

Lew Eisenberg, you encouraged me to be myself. Although I didn't run for office like you wanted, you must have thought that being who I am would have made a difference.

Cara Fish, thanks for your unbelievable devotion to this book and this project. Charlie Gasparino, thanks for introducing me to Todd—you never know!

And it goes without saying, a special thank you to Joe Califano for writing the Foreword and your seasoned feedback. For your support and inspiration.

People along the way, some mentioned and some not, who have accepted and encouraged me to be myself and write this book. Every time you listened or offered your opinion it fueled the fire.

All of the author's proceeds from the sale of this book will be donated to two worthy organizations: **CASA Columbia**, an organization that focuses on alcohol, tobacco, and drug use, abuse, and addiction, and assembles under one roof the skills needed to assess the impact of all addictive substances in all sectors of society; and the **Make-A-Wish Foundation**, especially the Samuel and Josephine Plumeri Wishing Place located in Monroe, New Jersey, which was opened in 2011 and named for the author's parents, providing families an environment that stimulates the imagination and reveals to seriously ill children the imaginative possibilities of a wish.

You can learn more about these two non-profits at www.casacolumbia.org and www.nj.wish.org.

Photo by Alan Schindler

Index

Acela Express, 129, 130
Addison, John, 102–103, 106, 109, 111, 113–114, 115, 117
A.L. Williams (company), 100–104, 113
See also Primerica
Albany Senators, 164
Alcatraz, 75
Alcohol abuse, 75, 150
Allen, Woody, 134
"Always show up," 122–123, 127, 132, 134, 145
See also Play in Traffic (Principle 6)
"Amazing Grace," 3
American Dream, 31–32, 128
American Express, 82
American Idol (TV show), 154
"*Amerika steht nicht allein*" ("America does not stand alone"), 3
Anorexia, 69, 73–74
Aon (company), 16

"Apostle" of life insurance, 112
Applying the Principles. *See* Principles
Arrogance, confidence and, 124
Asimov, Isaac, 152
Associated Press article, 150–151

Barger, Steve, 116
Barnes, Ronnie, 104
Barnstorming, 52
Baseball
Albany Senators, 164
Albany stadium project, 164–166
Binghamton Mets, 66
Blackball Stars (Holway), 53
Brooklyn Dodgers, 57–58
Clark, Tony, 63
at College of William and Mary, 34–35
fastball pitcher, 34
immigrants and, 49–50
junk ball pitcher, 35
Mays, Willie, 59, 67

Neshaminy High School coach, 37
New York Giants, 55
North Trenton Little League, 33
Philadelphia A's, 56–57
Pittsburgh Pirates, 52
Plumeri, Salvatore (grandfather of Joe Plumeri) and, 51–55
"Plumeri" baseball jersey, 28
racial divide, 57–58
Redding, Cannonball Dick, 53
Robinson, Jackie, 49, 57–59, 68, 137
Roland Garros Stadium, 5
"Run hard!" encouragement, 33, 35, 37
Trenton Giants, 55, 59, 67
Trenton Thunder (stadium and team), 59–68, 114
Yankee Stadium, 52, 56, 185
See also Dodgers; Yankees

Be yourself
  Be Yourself move-
    ment, 193
  checklist, 195
  courage and faith to
    be yourself, 4–5,
    68, 123
Bear Stearns, 6
Belief + Passion +
  Vision = Purpose,
  199
Bellizzi, Bob, 164, 165
Bernanke, Ben, 96
Big investor-little
  investor story,
  182–184
Bilardello, Carmine,
  96–98
Binghamton Mets, 66
Bisignano, Frank, 177
Blackball Stars (Hol-
  way), 53
Blankfein, Lloyd, 161
Boca Raton, 105, 106
Boies, David, 160
British Royal Marines,
  17
Brokerage firm-law
  firm confusion,
  38–40, 123–124,
  145
Brooklyn Dodgers. See
  Dodgers
Brown, Henry B. R.,
  184
Brown, James, 111
Bruno, Antonio, 141
Bruno, Gerardo, 141
Buckingham Palace, 2
Burger King, 142
Bush, George W., 96
Business Week article,
  112–113

Califano, Joe,
  150–152

Calls, returning,
  132–133
Calvin, Susan (fictional
  character), 152
Campanella, Roy, 57
Car dealership, 87
Carter, Jimmy, 150,
  151
Caruso, Joe, 63, 64, 65
CEOs
  octogenarian,
    136–137
  positive thinking,
    12, 20
  revolving door of,
    106–107
Chairman's lift, 8
Chamber of Com-
  merce, local, 142
Checklists
  being yourself, 195
  cutting your own
    path, 196
  play in traffic, 146
Cheers (TV show), 141
Chef training, 81–84
Childlike enthusiasm,
  144–145
China
  Peace Hotel in
    Shanghai, 27–28
  Three Gorges Dam,
    123
Chinese Brokers Asso-
  ciation, 27–28
Chirac, Jacques, 2
Chopra, Deepak, 4
Christian Plumeri
  Sports Complex,
  166
Churchill, Winston,
  148
Cigarette smoking,
  150–152
Citigroup, 5, 6, 174
Clark, Tony, 64

Clark, William R., 53
Clark's Lamb Works,
  51
Cogan, Berlind, Weill,
  and Levitt, 38–39,
  123, 181, 182–184
College of Saint Rose
  commencement
  address, 162–166
College of William and
  Mary, 5, 34–35, 37
Collins, Kathryn, 17
Columbus Club, 83
Columbus Day Parade,
  New York, 87
Columbus Foundation,
  136
Confidence, arrogance
  and, 124
Continental Airlines,
  99
Conventions,
  Primerica
  Georgia Dome con-
    ventions, 109–110,
    111, 118, 149
  Philadelphia Conven-
    tion Center, 111,
    112
Corvette incident, 78
Corzine, Jon, 88
Courage
  Churchill on, 148
  courage and faith to
    be yourself, 4–5,
    68, 123
  fighting for, 120
  of Jackie Robinson,
    58, 68
  moxie, 40, 123
Credit cards, illegal,
  79
Culinary Institute of
  America, 81–84
Cut Your Own Path
  (Principle 3), 47–68

application of, 196
checklist, 196
Robinson, Jackie, 49,
  57–59, 68, 137
Ruth, Babe, 49–50,
  52–54, 61, 81, 122
Trenton Thunder
  (baseball stadium
  and team), 59–68,
  114
See also Plumeri,
  Salvatore

Danbury federal cor-
  rectional institu-
  tion, 79–80
Danish people's reac-
  tion, World Trade
  Center, 3
Danson, Ted, 141
Darrow, Clarence,
  55, 56
Derek Jeter incident,
  185–186
Detroit Tigers, 63
DiMaggio, Joe (Joltin'
  Joe), 11, 55, 56
DirecTV, 113
Dodgers, Brooklyn
  Robinson, Jackie, 49,
  57–59, 68, 137
  Yankees and, 57–58
Drug addiction
  Fair Oaks Hospital,
  74–75
  manipulation and, 76
  Sara (girlfriend of
  Chris Plumeri),
  86–90
  Secret Harbor, 75–76
  self-esteem and, 69,
  72, 91
  See also Plumeri,
  Chris (older son of
  Joe Plumeri)
Dunn Field, 55

Dwyer, William F., 151

Ebbets Field, 56, 57
E-dating, 143–144
Ego, greed, willingness
  to please, 111–112,
  180–181
Eisenberg, Lew, 6
Electrical Porcelain
  Workers Union
  Local No. 266, 51
Elizabeth (daughter
  of Chris Plumeri),
  86–87
Élysée Palace, 6
Emotion, purpose and,
  174–176, 179–180
Engagement, with life,
  107, 125, 133, 137,
  139, 145
Enlarged heart, 90
Epilogue, 191–193
Esquire magazine, 135
Eure, Bryan, 160
Everyone Has the
  Same Plumbing
  (Principle 1), 1–28
  application of, 195
  checklist to being
  yourself, 195
  Chinese Brokers
  Association speech,
  27–28
  courage and faith to
  be yourself, 4–5,
  68, 123
  high-fiving each
  other, 17–18
  Plumeri's experiences
  at Willis, 6–27
  uniting impact of
  9/11 terrorist
  attacks, 1–4, 26
  See also Willis
  (insurance broker-
  age firm)

Facebook, 125, 192
Fair Oaks Hospital,
  74–75
Farleigh Dickinson
  University, 78
Fast food mania,
  141–142
Fastball pitcher, 34
Fear, leadership and,
  153–154
Feeling, 120
Feminism, Steinem
  and, 134–135
Fender Stratocaster, 32
Financial crisis of
  2008–2009, 95–96,
  126
Financial Needs Anal-
  ysis, 115–116
First Data, 174,
  177–180, 181,
  186–187
Florida, 59, 105, 106,
  155
Fonzi, 14
Ford, Betty, 69, 71,
  72
Ford, Jerry (Gerald
  Ford), 69, 71
Four Seasons Hotel,
  160

Garden State Baseball
  Limited Partner-
  ship, 67
Gays. See Same-sex
  marriages
Gehrig, Lou, 52, 53,
  61
George, David Lloyd,
  8
Georgia Dome con-
  ventions, 109–110,
  111, 118, 149
Georgia State Univer-
  sity, 102

Germany
  author's speech,
    laughing Germans,
    27
  Tiergarten Park gath-
    ering, 3
Gertler, Mark, 96
Glasco, George, 53
Go take the meeting!,
  122, 132
Goldman Sachs, 161
Googling passion, 147
Great Recession of
  2008–2009, 95–96,
  126
Greed, ego, willing-
  ness to please,
  111–112, 180–181
Grisham, John, 191
Gym incident, 78–79

Handwritten notes
  ("Joe notes"),
  138–139
Hazing, 50–51
Hearn, Steve, 22
Heart
  enlarged heart, 90
  inspiration and, 172
  listening to your
    heart, 162, 167
  quintuple bypass sur-
    gery, 59, 60, 106
  See also Make Your
    Heart Your Tele-
    prompter (Principle
    7)
Helicopter pilot inci-
  dent, 118–119
Heroes, inspiration
  and, 135
Hib, Rogal & Hobbs
  (HRH), 95–97
High on Arrival (Phil-
  lips), 75
High-fiving each other,
  17–18

Holway, John, 53
Hope, vision and,
  29–30
Hotels
  Four Seasons Hotel,
    160
  Peace Hotel, 27–28
  Waldorf Astoria
    Hotel dinner inci-
    dent, 87–89
  Wyndham hotel, 65
"How ya doin'?," 9,
  23, 105
HRH. *See* Hib, Rogal
  & Hobbs
Human Rights Cam-
  paign, 161
Humans, robots and,
  152–153

I Robot (Asimov), 152
I Robot (film), 152
Illegal credit cards, 79
Immigrants
  baseball and, 49–50
  hazing, 50–51
  See also Plumeri, Sal-
    vatore (grandfather
    of Joe Plumeri)
Incrementalists,
  172–173
Inspiration
  heart power and, 172
  heroes, 135
  motivational speak-
    ing *versus*, 119
  of own father, 115
  Primerica and, 100,
    104
Internet usage, 125,
  143–144
Intrepid Sea, Air and
  Space Museum, 89
iPad, First Data speech
  and, 186–187
IPO
  Primerica, 117

Willis (insurance
  brokerage firm),
  15, 16

James, Lebron, 154
Jay Z, 154
Jaycees, 142
Jennings, Jerry, 165
Jersey Shore (TV
  series), 79
Jeter, Derek, 185–186
Jim's story, 133–134
Job well done, 47
Joe Califano incident,
  150–152
"Joe notes," 138–139
Joe-isms, 17
joeplumeri.com, 192
John A. Roebling's
  Sons Company, 50
Joltin' Joe. *See* DiMag-
  gio, Joe
Junk ball pitcher, 35

Kennedy, Robert F., 74
KFC, 142
Kiwanis Club, 142
KKR. *See* Kohlberg,
  Kravis, Roberts
  & Co.
Knowledge, passion
  and, 62
  See also Passion
Kohlberg, Kravis,
  Roberts & Co.
  (KKR), 6, 10, 16
Krauze, Vic, 12
Kravis, Henry, 6–7,
  11, 140

Law firm-brokerage
  firm confusion,
  38–40, 123–124,
  145
Le Monde, 2
Leadership
  absence of, 107

chairman's lift and, 8

fear and, 153–154

listening and, 107

physics of, 21

relationships and, 197

Leonsis, Ted, 128–130

Lesbians. *See* Same-sex marriages

Let Sadness Teach You (Principle 4), 69–94

application of, 197

See also Plumeri, Chris (older son of Joe Plumeri)

Levine, Peter, 24–25

Life insurance

"apostle" of, 112

term life insurance, 101, 103

whole life insurance, 101, 104

See also Primerica; Willis

Life of Georgia, 102, 103

Lifecycle, 79

Lilly Oros incident, 55–56

Lions Club, 142

Listening

with focus, 197

leadership and, 107

to your heart, 162, 167

Little, Floyd, 34

Little investor-big investor story, 182–184

Loman, Willie (fictional character), 116

London company. *See* Willis (insurance brokerage firm)

Long hair, 76–77

Look Up, Not Down (Principle 5), 95–120

application of, 197–198

Hib, Rogal & Hobbs, 95–97

Sears Tower, 97–100, 131, 181–182

Willis Tower, 98–99, 131, 181–182

See also Primerica

Macaroni factory, 50

Mack, Connie, 56

Maître d', at Metropolitan Opera restaurant, 83–84

Make Your Heart Your Teleprompter (Principle 7), 147–167

application of, 198

College of Saint Rose commencement address, 162–166

father-daughter relations (Joe Plumeri and Leslie), 158–159

father-son relations (Joe Plumeri and Jay), 155–158

Googling passion, 147

Joe Califano incident, 150–152

partner benefits, 159

robots and humans, 152–153

same-sex marriages, 160–162

St. Rose baseball stadium project, 164–166

Teleprompter society, 149

Malone, Puggy, 33

Malone, Sam (fictional character), 141

Maloney, Jim, 63

Manipulation, drug addiction and, 76

Marsh (company), 16

Mays, Willie, 59, 67

McDonald's, 65, 142

MetLife, 98

Metropolitan Opera restaurant, 83–84

Mexico City Summer Olympics, 37

Microphone usage, 113–114

Minor league baseball. *See* Trenton Thunder (baseball stadium and team)

Moinian, Joe, 97

Money market fund, 184

Motivational speaking, inspiration and, 119

Moxie, 40, 123

Ms. magazine, 134, 135

Murderers' Row, 52

NBC Evening News, 99

Needs-based selling, 115–116

Neglect, 93

Neshaminy High School, 37

New Jersey Tile Company, 51

New York Giants, 55

New York Law School, 37–38

New York Playboy Club, 134–135

New York Times, 54, 66, 67, 161

New York Yankees. *See* Yankees

New York's Columbus Day Parade, 87

Newcombe, Don, 57

9/11 attacks. *See* September 11, 2001 terrorist attacks

Nixon, Richard, 37

"No," "on" and, 125

Normandy Beach visit, 7–8

North Trenton Little League, 33

Nous sommes tous Américains ("We are all Americans"), 2

Obi-Wan Kenobi, 175

Octogenarian CEOs, 136–137

Office of Supervisory Jurisdiction, 115

"On," "no" and, 125

One Day at a Time (TV sitcom), 75

Open-door policy, 42, 137–138

Optimism. *See* Positive thinking

Oros, Lilly, 55–56

Outward Bound program, 158–159

Padgett, Gerald, 102–103

"Pajamas" story, 19

Paris, 5–6

Partner benefits, 159

Passion
feeling and, 120
Googling, 147
knowledge and, 62
as purpose plus emotion, 174–176, 179–180

Vision + Belief + Passion = Purpose, 199

Pasucci, Chris, 118–119

Peace Hotel, 27–28

"Pennies from Heaven," 36, 37

Pentagon terrorist attacks, 2

Philadelphia A's, 56–57

Philadelphia Convention Center, 111, 112

Phillies. *See* Philadelphia A's

Phillips, Mackenzie, 75

Physical trainer, 84

Physics, of leadership, 21

Picture Perfect Weight Loss series (Shapiro), 85

Pins, at Willis, 17–19

Pitchers, baseball, 34–35

Pittsburgh Pirates, 52

Play in Traffic (Principle 6), 121–146
"always show up," 122–123, 127, 132, 134, 145
application of, 198
childlike enthusiasm, 144–145
Columbus Foundation speech, 136
engagement with life, 107, 125, 133, 137, 139, 145
Go take the meeting!, 122, 132
Internet usage compared to, 125, 143–144
Jim's story, 133–134
list of activities, 146

local community involvement, 142

octogenarian CEOs, 136–137

Plumeri, Salvatore (grandfather of Joe Plumeri), 127–128

religious gathering places, 142–143

returning calls, 132–133

risk taking, 121–122, 144

Ristorante San Pietro experience, 140–141

ship metaphor, 131

Steinem, Gloria, 134–135

Ted Leonsis incident, 128–130

variations on, 130–131

Yichang meeting, 123

Playboy bunnies, 134–135

Plumeri, Chris (older son of Joe Plumeri), 70 (photo)
anorexia of, 69, 73–74
birth of, 73
car dealership jobs and, 87
chef training, 81–84
Christian Plumeri Sports Complex and, 166
Corvette incident, 78
at Danbury federal correctional institution, 79–80
death of, 90–91, 95, 166
Elizabeth (daughter of Chris Plumeri), 86–87

enlarged heart of, 90
at Fair Oaks Hospital, 74–75
at Farleigh Dickinson University, 78
father's lack of help, 72–73
father's regrets about relationship, 91–94
Ford's letter to, 71
gym incident, 78–79
illegal credit cards incident, 79
long hair issue, 76–77
as maître d' at Metropolitan Opera restaurant, 83–84
marriage to Stephanie, 85–86
physical trainer aspirations, 84
Sara (girlfriend of Chris Plumeri), 86–90
at Secret Harbor, 75–76
self-esteem, 69, 72, 91
sensitivity of, 72, 77
Shapiro's relation with, 85
Waldorf Astoria Hotel dinner incident, 87–89
Plumeri, Jay (younger son of Joe Plumeri)
best man at Chris's wedding, 85
father's lack of help, 73
father's relationship with, 155–158
Plumeri restaurant, 157–158
Race Lane restaurant, 158

Waldorf Astoria Hotel dinner incident, 88–89
wedding, 156
Plumeri, Joseph J., II
brokerage firm-law firm confusion, 38–40, 123–124, 145
Business Week article on, 112–113
calls to top 100 executives at Willis, 11–12
Chris's relationship with, 91–94
Jay's relationship with, 155–158
lack of help to children, 72–73
Lilly Oros incident, 55–56
missed opportunities with Chris, 76–77
moxie of, 40, 123
at Primerica, 100–120
Trenton Thunder stadium assistance, 63–65
at Willis, 6–27
See also Willis
Plumeri, Leslie (daughter of Joe Plumeri)
at Chris's wedding, 85
father's lack of help, 73
Outward Bound program, 158–159
Plumeri, Nancy (first wife of Joe Plumeri)
birth (of Chris Plumeri), 73
Kravis's meeting with, 6
parenting

responsibilities, 73
in Paris, 5–6
Plumeri, Paul (youngest brother of Joe Plumeri), 32
Plumeri, Salvatore (grandfather of Joe Plumeri)
Babe Ruth and, 52, 61
baseball and, 51–55
death, 47
funeral, 47, 49
life, 50–52
playing in traffic, 127–128
in *Prominent Families of New Jersey*, 50–51
quintuple bypass surgery, 59, 60, 106
Plumeri, Sam (brother of Joe Plumeri), 32, 62–63
Plumeri, Samuel (father of Joe Plumeri)
death, 115
Lilly Oros incident, 55–56
positive thinking of, 29, 32, 36–37
at Primerica, 114–115
"Run hard!" encouragement, 33, 35, 37
Trenton Thunder (stadium and team), 59–68, 114
Plumeri, Stephanie (wife of Chris Plumeri), 85–86
Plumeri, Susan (wife of Joe Plumeri), 132, 155, 156
Plumeri restaurant, 157–158

Port of Authority
Building, 8
Positive thinking
of Ford, Betty, 69
of Plumeri, Samuel,
29, 32, 36–37
Sears Tower incident,
97–100
of Willis CEO, 12,
20
Primerica
Addison, John,
102–103, 106, 109,
111, 113–114, 115,
117
A.L. Williams (com-
pany), 100–104,
113
Barger, Steve, 116
Barnes, Ronnie, 104
Business Week arti-
cle, 112–113
DirecTV, 113
founding, 100–101
Georgia Dome con-
ventions, 109–110,
111, 118, 149
inspiration and, 100,
104
IPO, 117
mission of, 100
needs-based selling,
115–116
Office of Supervisory
Jurisdiction, 115
Padgett, Gerald,
102–103
Philadelphia Conven-
tion Center, 111,
112
Plumeri, Joe,
100–120
Plumeri, Samuel,
114–115
revolving door of
CEOs, 106–107

satellite network,
113–114
Weill, Sandy,
104–105
Williams, Art,
100–104, 106, 113
Williams, Rick, 117
Princess Leia, 175
Principles
application of,
195–199
Cut Your Own Path,
47–68
Everyone Has the
Same Plumbing,
1–28
Let Sadness Teach
You, 69–94
Look Up, Not Down,
95–120
Make Your Heart
Your Teleprompter,
147–167
Play in Traffic,
121–146
review of, 170–172
Show the Way to
Grandma's House,
29–45
You Gotta Have Pur-
pose, 169–190
Prominent Families of
New Jersey, 50–51
Purpose
emotion and,
174–176, 179–180
Vision + Belief + Pas-
sion = Purpose,
199
See also You Gotta
Have Purpose
(Principle 8)

Quintuple bypass sur-
gery, 59, 60, 106

Race Lane restaurant,
158
Racial divide, 57–58
Rau, Johannes, 3
Redding, Cannonball
Dick, 53
Relationships
advice on, 93–94
leadership and, 197
Religious gathering
places, 142–143
Returning calls,
132–133
Revolving door, of
CEOs, 106–107
Risk taking, 121–122,
144
See also Play in Traf-
fic (Principle 6)
Ristorante San Pietro,
140–141
Robinson, Jackie, 49,
57–59, 68, 137
Robinson, Jim, 82
Robinson, Rachel, 137
Robots, humans and,
152–153
Rockwell, Norman,
51
Roland Garros Sta-
dium, 5
Romney, Mitt,
148–149, 154
Roosevelt Boulevard,
56
Rotary Club, 142
Rue du Fau-
bourg-Saint-Hon-
oré, 6
"Run hard!," 33, 35,
37
Ruth, Babe, 49–50,
52–54, 61, 81, 122

Same-sex marriages,
160–162

Sara (girlfriend of Chris Plumeri), 86–90
Satellite network, Primerica and, 113–114
Sears Tower, 97–100, 131, 181–182
Secret Harbor, 75–76
Securities and Exchange Commission, 184
Self-esteem, 69, 72, 91
Sensitivity, of Chris Plumeri, 72, 77
September 11, 2001 terrorist attacks (9/11)
  Chopra's message, 4
  Pentagon, 2
  Plumeri restaurant and, 157
  Twin Towers, 2–3
  uniting impact of, 1–4, 26
  World Trade Center, 2–3, 157
Shangahi, Peace Hotel in, 27–28
Shapiro, Howard, 85
Shearson Lehman Brothers, 76, 129, 177
Shibe Park, 56
Ship metaphor, 131
Show magazine, 134
Show the Way to Grandma's House (Principle 2), 29–45
  application of, 195–196
  law firm-brokerage firm confusion, 38–40, 123–124, 145

vision, 29–30, 33, 41–45
See also Plumeri, Samuel (father of Joe Plumeri)
"Showing up," 122–123, 127, 132, 134, 145
See also Play in Traffic (Principle 6)
Sinatra, Frank, 55, 56
Skype, First Data speech and, 186–187
"Slow-motion suicide," cigarette smoking, 150–151
Smith, Will, 152
Smith Barney, 116
Smoking cigarettes, 150–152
Sollami, Mrs., 31
Sollami, Paul, 33
St. Rose baseball stadium project, 164–166
Stadiums. See Baseball
Star-Spangled Banner, 2
Steinbrenner, George, 63
Steinem, Gloria, 134–135
Stock market crash of 1987, 153
Stout, David, 66–67
Sullivan, Mark, 165–166

Tax Equity and Fiscal Responsibility Act of 1981, 101
"T-Bone Shuffle," 32
Technicolor, 167
Ted Leonsis incident, 128–130

"Telepresence" rooms, 174–175
Teleprompter society, 149
See also Make Your Heart Your Teleprompter (Principle 7)
Television (TV)
  American Idol (TV show), 154
  Cheers (TV show), 141
  DirecTV, 113
  Jersey Shore (TV series), 79
  One Day at a Time (TV sitcom), 75
Term life insurance, 101, 103
Terrorism, 33, 97
See also September 11, 2001 terrorist attacks
Three Gorges Dam, 123
Tiergarten Park, 3
Tobacco Institute, 151
Tower of London, 8
Tower Room, 13
Transformationalists, 172–173
Transistor radios, 56–57
Trenton Catholic Boys High School, 33
Trenton Giants, 55, 59, 67
Trenton Thunder (baseball stadium and team), 59–68, 114
Trenton Times article, 52–53
Truman, Harry, 149
TV. See Television

Twin Towers, 2–3
Twitter @JJPlumeri,
192

United Airlines, 99
University of Georgia,
102
US Junior Chamber,
142

"Value gap," 116
Villalba, Sicily, 47, 85
Villalba Club, 47–48
Vision
feeling and, 120
hope and, 29–30
Show the Way to
Grandma's House,
29–30, 33, 41–45
Vision + Belief + Passion = Purpose, 199
See also Show the
Way to Grandma's
House (Principle 2)

Waldorf Astoria Hotel
dinner incident,
87–89
Washington Capitals,
128
Washington Wizards,
128
Waterfront Park, 66,
115
See also Trenton
Thunder
"We are all Americans" (Nous
sommes tous
Américains), 2
Weddings, 85, 155,
156, 160, 162
Weill, Sandy, 39–40,
41, 104–105, 107,
123–124, 145

Wetzel Field, 52, 53
White, Bill, 160
Whole life insurance,
101, 104
William and Mary,
College of, 5, 34, 37
Williams, Art, 100–
104, 106, 113
Williams, Brian, 99
Williams, Rick, 117
Willingness to
please, ego, greed,
111–112, 180–181
Willis (insurance brokerage firm)
Aon and, 16
handwritten notes
("Joe notes"),
138–139
IPO, 15, 16
Kravis, H. and, 6–7,
11, 140
location of, 8
Marsh and, 16
open-door policy,
42, 137–138
partner benefits, 159
pins at, 17–19
Plumeri, Joe, and,
6–27
Plumeri's calls to top
100 executives,
11–12
same-sex marriages,
160–161
"telepresence"
rooms, 174–175
Tower Room, 13
Willis Tower, 98–99,
131, 181–182
Willy Loman selling,
116
Winfrey, Oprah, 135
World Series, 52, 57,
58

World Trade Center
terrorist attacks,
2–3, 157
Wyndham hotel, 65

Yangtze River, 123
Yankee Stadium, 52,
56, 185
Yankees
Brooklyn Dodgers
and, 57–58
DiMaggio, Joe, 11,
55, 56
Gehrig, Lou, 52,
53, 61
Jeter, Derek,
185–186
Ruth, Babe, 49–50,
52–54, 61, 81, 122
Steinbrenner,
George, 63
World Series, 52,
57, 58
Yichang meeting, 123
You Gotta Have Purpose (Principle 8),
169–190
application, 199
big investor-little
investor story,
182–184
Derek Jeter incident,
185–186
First Data experiences, 174,
177–180, 181,
186–187
purpose and emotion, 174–176,
179–180
purpose statement,
189–190
willingness to please,
111–112, 180–181